Complicated Losses, Difficult Deaths

A Practical Guide
For Ministering to Grievers

Roslyn A. Karaban, PhD

Resource Publications, Inc.
San Jose, California

Reprint Department
Resource Publications, Inc.
160 E. Virginia Street #290
San Jose, CA 95112-5876
(408) 286-8505 (voice)
(408) 287-8748 (fax)

Library of Congress Cataloging-in-Publication Data
Karaban, Roslyn A.
   Complicated losses, difficult deaths: a practical guide for
   ministering to grievers /
Roslyn A. Karaban.
      p. cm.
   Includes bibliographical references and index.
   ISBN 0-89390-476-7 (pbk.)
   1. Grief—Religious aspects—Christianity. 2. Pastoral
   counseling—Case studies. I. Title.
BV4905.2.K37 1999
259'.6—dc21   99-051391

Printed in the United States of America.
04 03 02 01 00 | 5 4 3 2 1

Editorial director: Nick Wagner
Prepress manager: Elizabeth Asborno
Project coordinator: Mike Sagara
Copyeditor: Robin Witkin
Indexer: Sylvia Coates

Author photograph by Leichtner Studios, Inc.

Dedicated in memory of my parents and father-in-law —
all difficult deaths.

Their deaths, and lives, were my greatest teachers.

Regina Rita McGinn Steinbacher Karaban (1915–1975)
William John Karaban (1911–1993)
Easter Rakshanya Das (1917–1997)

Contents

Preface. vii

Acknowledgments ix

Introduction: What Is Complicated Grief? 1

Uncomplicated Grief 1

Complicated Grief 6

Complicated Losses, Difficult Deaths 6

Study Questions and Practicum 11

Chapter One: Ambiguous Losses 13

Alzheimer's Disease 16

Divorce 25

Study Questions and Practicums 30

Chapter Two: Disenfranchised Losses 33

Suicide 35

AIDS 43

Abortion 50

Study Questions and Practicums 53

Chapter Three: Sudden, Unanticipated Losses 55

Sudden Death: Accident 58

Sudden Death: Homicide 65

Rape 68

Study Questions and Practicums 71

Chapter Four: Children and Death 73

Parental Loss of a Child 73

Death of a Sibling 80

Loss of a Parent 85

Study Questions and Practicums. 87

Chapter Five: Lingering Losses. 89

Complicated Death from Cancer 90

Mental Illness 95

Multiple Sclerosis 97

Study Questions and Practicums 100

Chapter Six: Caring for Grief Ministers 103

Practicums 110

Appendix

Skills. 111

Empathy
Summary
Focusing
Prompts
Probes
Information Questions
Information Sharing
Self-Disclosure
Advanced Empathy
Immediacy

Drawing Grief 118

Endnotes. 119

Bibliography 125

Preface

This has been my most difficult book to write. Although the content flowed easily from my many years of teaching, counseling, and working with grief, I was not prepared for the emotional heaviness I would experience from living with and writing about such difficult and tragic losses. As much as I tried to remain detached from my writing and did not use actual case material, I was continually reminded of and drawn into my own grief and the grief of people who have actually experienced similar losses. As I wrote this book my church community experienced the resignation, firing, and removal of *fourteen* staff members. No matter how I tried to hide from my own grief, *grief found me*.

My most poignant experience came as I was writing the chapter on sudden, unanticipated losses. I became quite engrossed in my story of George and Susan and was feeling quite proud of my fictional writing abilities. Needing to take a break I wandered over to the classroom building and ran into a former student. When she asked me how I was, I immediately began sharing with her my excitement about how my story of George and Susan was developing. As I talked, I could see she did not share in my excitement. Sensing something was wrong, I asked her how *she* was. She shared with me that her closest friend had just died the day before after many months of illness. She was struggling with this death and with ministering to her friend's husband of forty years who was lost without his life partner. I was brought back to the reality of actual losses that continue to invade our lives. I saw this as a reminder that for many people reading this book, the stories of loss will be all too painful and all too real. This was a difficult, but necessary reminder. I had been trying to live in a world where the losses were not real. I needed to be reminded that no matter how I try to escape from the reality of loss, *grief will find me*.

The name of this book came partly from a talk I gave in February 1996. I was asked to speak on "Difficult Deaths" and told the deaths I was to address were suicide, AIDS-related deaths, sudden death, and the death of children. I gave a very well researched and thorough lunchtime talk to more than one hundred people, listing the many characteristics of each type of grief, and how we can better minister and counsel in these difficult situations. Most of the people in the audience were hospice workers—chaplains, nurses, and volunteers. The talk was well received and many told me how helpful it was. Moments after the talk finished I was approached by a middle-aged couple. "We're the Smiths," they informed me, clearly indicating I should know who they were. I didn't have a clue. "Yes," I replied, trying to sound open and encouraging. "You must have read about us in the newspaper," they continued. I tried to recall major news stories of the past few days. "We came here because we are experiencing a difficult death, but you didn't talk about it today." Hadn't I covered the major difficult deaths? What could they have experienced? I wondered. "We are grieving the death of Molly—she was going to be our daughter-in-law—and she was murdered ... by our son. He is now in prison for her murder. Not only have we lost Molly, whom we loved dearly, but we have also lost our son. Can you help us?" No matter how hard I try to be objective about or detached from grief, *grief finds me*.

God has a way of bringing people into my life to remind me that the pain of grief—particularly complicated grief—is enormous, and is within me and around me at all times. This book is written in the hope that it may help the grieving and those who minister with the grieving[1] to live in and get through this pain a little better.

Acknowledgments

This book draws on more than a decade of teaching and counseling experience and more than four decades of my life experience. In particular I would like to acknowledge and thank the many people who have been my teachers and my supporters in grief ministry:

• my parents, Regina and Bill, to whom this book is dedicated

• my husband, Prem, who continues to be my loving, life partner in good times and bad

• my best friend, Nancy Stetson Wrobel, who continues to suffer with me in my grief and celebrate with me in my joy

• my colleagues at Samaritan Pastoral Counseling Center, especially John Karl, Trevor Watt, and Lucinda Wilcox, who have worked with me in developing a training program for hospice chaplains and who have supported me in my accreditation process in death education and grief therapy

• my colleagues at St. Bernard's Institute, especially President Patricia Schoelles, who continues to encourage me in my work

• my students and clients and friends who continue to privilege me with their stories of grief, especially the students of my "Ministering in Loss, Death, and Grief" classes

• my editor, Nick Wagner, and the production staff at Resource Publications, Inc., who continue to have faith in my writing and who continue to make that writing better through their careful editing and arrangement

Introduction

What Is Complicated Grief?

Uncomplicated Grief

Whenever we experience a *significant* loss, our internal reaction is one of *grief*. We can't experience a significant loss without also experiencing grief. Grief is an unavoidable, spontaneous response to loss. Grief is universal—felt by everyone—and is experienced at many and varied times in our lives. It is an ordinary, everyday occurrence that we all must live through.

Grief is also unique to each individual. *How* we experience grief and *what* we experience in our grief differs from person to person, circumstance to circumstance, and culture to culture. No two experiences of grief are ever exactly the same. Yet there are some commonalities in our experiences, and it is these commonalities that draw us together in our grief. For most of us, grief evolves into a process of *grieving* that stays with us over time and consists of certain responses[1] and accompanying tasks.

Initial Responses

Psychological: shock, denial, and disbelief. After experiencing a significant loss such as the death of a loved one, a divorce, or the sudden loss of a job, our initial emotional reaction is usually disbelief, even shock. We can't believe that this has actually happened to us. Our loved one is not dead, or gone; we have not been fired or downsized. We simply cannot and will not believe that this event has taken place. This disbelief may occur even if the loss is anticipated. It is our way of adapting to the impact that the loss has and will continue to have on us, and of cushioning the initial blow of immediate, unrelenting pain. This is an automatic and natural response that allows us additional time to adapt, particularly to the overall and everyday psychological, social, and spiritual ramifications of the loss.

Physical: loss of weight, crying, inability to sleep, lack of strength, and physical exhaustion. This list of physical responses represents only some of the possibilities. These responses may continue throughout the grieving process, and seem to be the least under our control. Our physical responses often create the greatest anxiety in our grieving process and are of the most immediate concern to us.

Social/Behavioral: dependency, detachment, and avoidance of being alone. Again, this is not an exhaustive list. Initially, our social response is to detach from social activity while desiring the companionship and support of others. Behaviorally, we become forgetful and find we act ineffectively and unproductively at work, at home, and in social situations.

Spiritual: insecurity, confusion, distrust, anger, and questioning. We question God's steadfastness and faithfulness, and even God's very existence. We question God's actions in our lives. We may ask, Why did God do this? We may wonder if we are being punished. Meaning eludes us.

Continuing Responses

We cannot remain in shock and disbelief for very long. All too soon the reality of loss sets in, and we enter what is described as the middle of the grieving process. This response to loss lasts the longest and is the hardest to get through. Erich Lindemann coined the phrase "grief work" to describe the process of getting through this time of grieving.

Psychological: disorganization and despair. Other feelings include confusion, yearning, sadness, anxiety, guilt, anger, relief, loneliness, resentment, emptiness, shame, helplessness, and hopelessness. We may feel overwhelmed and bombarded by the variety and intensity of our many feelings.

Physical: loss of weight, inability to sleep, decreased sexual interest, crying, fatigue, chest pains or palpitations, a lump in the throat or choking, and digestive problems. The physical responses of the initial response to loss continue and increase. Coupled with the emotional, social, and spiritual responses, these recurring physical responses can be quite distressing.

Social/Behavioral: restlessness, inability to initiate and maintain long periods of social activity, inability to sit still, and withdrawal from social activity. At the very time we need support and companionship the most, our social response is to withdraw. Other behavioral responses include hyperactivity, increased use of medication, disturbances in appetite and sleep patterns, a tendency to either cling or withdraw, and a tendency toward impulsive behaviors.

Spiritual: loneliness, a fear of being abandoned in our grief, and a need to be comforted, supported, and loved. We may ask, *Where* is God in our pain? *Who* is this God who has caused so much suffering? We desire the presence of God and the presence of others, yet often feel only their absence.

Culminating Responses

Although some losses will take a lifetime to grieve, there will come a time for most losses when the loss is no longer the primary focus, or the central preoccupation, of our lives. We transition back into the world of living.

Psychological: reorganization and reconnection. Eventually we are able to sufficiently work through many of our feelings of grief and to let go of (emotionally decathect from) our previous relationship with the deceased. We are ready to reconnect to a world without the physical presence of our loved one. We are able to reinvest in life and look to the future. There is a diminishment of our intermediate emotional responses and a renewed desire for living, although guilt about doing so may continue to bother us. We now find we are able to reconnect to the world.

Physical: return to pre-grief status, increased sensitivity and vulnerability. Although our life, including our physical health, will never be the same, the intensity and number of our intermediate physical grief responses will diminish. A severe intermediate physical response may occasionally occur, but it will be a temporary experience.[2] Our physical health may be somewhat weakened from the toll of working through the emotional, physical, social, and spiritual responses of intermediate grieving.

Social/Behavioral: reentry into the social world, establishment of a new identity, and trying out new behaviors. For many, this will be the hardest and most frightening part of the whole grieving process. We may be single for the first time in forty years, and wonder if we even want to *think* about dating again. This can be an *exciting* time also—a time to try new activities and form new friendships.

Spiritual: hopefulness, transformation, and resurrection. Hope is resurrected. Our relationship with God is being transformed. We begin to find God present in the midst of our anguish and angst. We are rediscovering God as a faithful, loving, and ever-present companion in our grief. We may once again proclaim God as a God who suffers with us, and as a God who has a preference for the grieving.[3]

Tasks

The tasks of grieving are related to the responses of grieving. The responses of grieving are *how* we experience our grief—physically, emotionally, socially, and spiritually. The tasks of grieving are what we need to *do* to get through our grieving. These tasks include (Tatelbaum 22; Worden 10–18; Parkes & Weiss 153–161):

- accepting and understanding that a loss has occurred (intellectually)
- experiencing and expressing the emotions and reactions of grief and accepting that a loss has occurred (emotionally)
- adjusting to an environment of loss
- letting go of the attachment to what was lost
- emotionally relocating the deceased
- assuming a new identity
- reinvesting in life

In spiritual terms, I would add the following tasks:

- working through our anger, confusion, and disbelief
- finding meaning in loss
- coming to a renewed understanding of who God is to us
- reconnecting to God
- resurrecting hope

Describing grief in terms of stages has come under a lot of criticism in recent times.[4] The implication of the concept of stages is that grief is linear and tidy and can be gotten through by following steps in a certain sequential order. We all know that this is not how we experience grief. Grieving is more spiral than linear, more of an unending circle than a progression of steps. Grief is anything but neat and orderly and often wreaks havoc in our lives.

I still find value in describing grieving in terms of broad *phases* of emotions and experiences, although I have come to prefer the terms "responses" or "reactions." There is a universality and a commonality to my grieving that *is* similar to your grieving. Identifying the "ordinary" path of grieving and the "usual" responses of grief helps grievers to feel less alone, less isolated, less afraid, and more connected to others.

Phase, stage, or response language is helpful as long as it is *descriptive* rather than *prescriptive*, and takes into account the variations that occur because of differing social, cultural, and religious contexts. Identifying common experiences of grieving—even in a broad way—helps grief ministers[5] to be better able to respond appropriately and adequately to grievers.

The type of grief just described is what may be referred to as *uncomplicated grieving*, or grieving that follows a somewhat predictable path. This does not mean it is not painful or difficult grieving or that it won't at times seem more circuitous than linear. But it is grief that we have all gotten through and grief that can more easily be ministered to. This type of grief used to be referred to as "normal" grief, but the implication is that all other grief is abnormal, a term that carries with it—even when accurate—an unnecessary, and even harmful stigma. It has also been called "little griefs" (Westberg 12), another term I prefer to avoid because of the response it may evoke in grievers or grief ministers. "Little griefs" may appear to be ones that are hardly worth worrying about. Yet even "little" losses need to be grieved. Actually, "little" losses *must* be grieved so we will be able to grieve what I refer to as the more *complicated losses*.

Complicated Grief

Losses that fall into the category of *complicated losses* evoke *complicated grief reactions.* These have also been known as abnormal, pathological, unresolved, and dysfunctional grief—to name a few of the earlier labels used. All these terms carry a negative, even derogatory connotation, which even when accurate can unnecessarily alienate grievers and prejudice or even frighten grief ministers. I prefer the terms "complicated loss" or "complicated grief" now being used in recent works on grief. These terms capture both the complexity of the loss experience and the implicit, unique challenges of the ensuing grieving and mourning experiences. These terms also avoid the potential association of mental or medical illness that previous terms too often denoted, and they provide grievers and grief ministers with a term that is accurate, hopeful, and indicative of difficulties that can be gotten through and ministered to.

I have struggled with using "complicated losses" because in my experience *any* loss and *any* death can be difficult or complicated, and it is not usually helpful to compare losses. However, in my counseling with the grieving, in my teaching and researching about grief, and in my own experience, I have become convinced that some deaths and some losses—by their very nature—are more complicated. These losses are more complicated because they evoke grief symptoms, grief reactions, and grief feelings that are more intense and that last longer than "ordinary" (uncomplicated) grief; therefore, grievers are less likely to be sufficiently supported in a sustained and healing way. These types of losses overwhelm the person's ability to accept, cope, and move on, and leave the griever stuck in grief or unable to grieve.

Although many books have been written on uncomplicated ordinary grief, few books have spent adequate time on complicated grief.[6] This book will do just that with the added dimension of focusing on those who *minister* in complicated grieving situations.

Complicated Losses, Difficult Deaths

A *complicated loss* is defined in one of two ways—either by the *type* of loss itself, or by *factors* surrounding the loss. When a complicated loss is a *death*, it is considered *complicated* or *difficult* when the type of death is (Rando, *Complicated Mourning* 7–10; Walsh and McGoldrick, "Loss and the Family" 13–18):

- sudden or unexpected
- violent (suicide, murder)
- mutilating
- that of a child
- the result of an overly lengthy illness

Losses that are considered complicated—by their very nature—yet do not always fall in the category of death include the following:

- ambiguous losses (Alzheimer's disease, addiction, and divorce)
- traumatic losses (abuse and community disasters)
- disenfranchised losses (children's grief and imprisonment)

This last type of complicated loss may involve an actual death (such as AIDS, suicide, or abortion) or a psychosocial death (such as mental illness or addiction).

The second way a loss is defined as complicated is by factors surrounding the loss or death itself. These factors include (Rando, *Complicated Mourning* 31–32; Walsh and McGoldrick, "Loss and the Family" 13–27):

- the type of relationship with the deceased or lost person — angry, ambivalent, dependent, conflicted, or estranged
- the type of family patterns surrounding the loss or death — enmeshed, disengaged, intolerant, or inflexible
- the type of family belief system surrounding the loss or death — condemning, blaming, shameful, or guilty
- the type of communication surrounding the loss — blocked or secret
- the lack of perceived family, social, economic, or faith resources
- the role of the lost person — only child, matriarch, favored child
- the untimeliness of the loss — death of a child, death after remission, or death after marriage
- the survivor's perception that the death or loss was preventable

- the presence of previous and present liabilities — other, concurrent losses or stressors
- mental illness
- multiple losses
- the presence of unacknowledged secondary losses — loss of hope, loss of faith, loss of income, or loss of companionship
- the inheritance of a legacy of unresolved loss, spanning across generations
- the context of the death — the relationship with the deceased is not recognized
- the loss is not recognized, the griever is not recognized (disenfranchised grief)
- the extent of the loss — a community disaster, a war, an epidemic

If any of these factors are present, the grieving may be difficult. Obviously, if multiple factors are present, there is even greater potential for difficulties in grieving.

When the very *nature* of the death is complicated, or when the *factors* surrounding the loss are complicated, the loss is considered complicated, and the grieving process that ensues *may* be complicated. *Complicated grief* [7] describes the complications that can occur in the unfolding of the grieving process after the loss has occurred. Another term that has been used to describe this complicated grief process is "unresolved grief." Therese Rando describes seven types of unresolved grief (*Grief, Dying and Death* 59–62):

1. *Absent grief* — The grieving process is absent; it is as if a loss never occurred.

2. *Inhibited grief* — There is an inhibition of the usual expression of grief, with the presence of somatic symptoms instead; grievers may only be able to mourn certain qualities of the deceased, such as their positive attributes.

3. *Delayed grief* — Grief is delayed up to years; a grief reaction may eventually be triggered by another loss.

4. *Conflicted (distorted) grief* — There is an exaggeration or distortion of one of the expressions of ordinary grief, particularly

an exaggeration of anger or guilt that may be prolonged; this often occurs after the death of a loved one with whom grievers had a dependent or ambiguous relationship.

5. *Chronic grief* — Grievers continue to manifest intense grief reactions, which would only be appropriate in the early part of grief; grieving is continuous and does not draw to any conclusion. Grievers experience an intense desire or yearning for the deceased or lost one. This type of grief is often present after the loss of a person on whom grievers were particularly dependent, or when grievers are especially insecure.

6. *Unanticipated grief* — This grief often occurs after a very sudden or unanticipated loss. It is characterized by a feeling of disruptiveness. Grievers cannot comprehend the full consequences of the loss. Grievers experience extreme feelings of bewilderment, anxiety, self-reproach, and depression and are unable to function in life. The symptoms of grief stay with grievers for a prolonged period of time.

7. *Abbreviated grief* — This grief is often mistaken for unresolved grief. It is short, but normal grief that may occur because of an immediate replacement of the lost person or relationship (remarriage), a lack of attachment to the lost person or relationship, or because adequate anticipatory grief has occurred.

Rando proposes that there can be complications in the mourning process if there is *any* "compromise, distortion, or failure" (*Complicated Mourning* 12) in what she delineates as the six "R" processes of mourning (45):

1. Recognize the loss

2. React to the separation

3. Recollect and reexperience the deceased and the relationship

4. Relinquish old attachments to the deceased and to the old assumptive world[8]

5. Readjust to move adaptively into the new world without forgetting the old

6. Reinvest

It is helpful to reorganize Rando's seven types of unresolved grief in relation to her six "R" processes of mourning. Each type of unresolved grief is now associated with a particular "R" process, which helps grief ministers to understand particular, potential difficulties in grieving (156):

- Absent and unanticipated mourning are now seen as interferences in the first "R" process — recognizing the loss.

- Delayed mourning, inhibited mourning, and conflicted mourning are now seen as interferences in the second "R" process — reacting to the loss.

- Inhibited mourning and conflicted or distorted mourning are now seen as interferences in the third "R" process — recollecting and reexperiencing the deceased and the relationship.

- Chronic mourning is now seen as an interference in the fourth and fifth "R" processes — relinquishing old attachments and readjusting to the new world.

The good news in all of this is, It is never too late to express grief or to learn how to (re)grieve.

In this book there is an emphasis on:

1. learning to be *aware* that certain losses may be complicated because of the very nature (type) of loss

2. gaining an understanding of complicated grief that can enhance the ability of grievers to grieve and grief ministers to provide pastoral care[9]

3. exploring actual situations and responses that can serve as a guide for grievers and grief ministers

Each chapter will look at different types of complicated losses noting some of the unique characteristics that accompany each loss, and will examine various possible responses based on these characteristics. Short case studies and pastoral conversations (mock verbatims[10]) will be used to illustrate and concretize a variety of experiences.

Study Questions

1. What is "ordinary" (uncomplicated) grief? What are the three basic responses or phases of grief? What are some of the tasks of grieving?

2. What is meant by "complicated grief"? What are the five types of death that are considered complicated by their very nature? What are other types of losses that may also be considered complicated?

3. What are some of the factors surrounding a death or loss that may also cause it to be considered complicated?

4. What are the seven types of unresolved grief?

5. What are the six "R" processes of mourning?

Practicum

Break the larger group into pairs (dyads). Have one person share a situation of ordinary grief with a partner. Switch roles. Have one person share a situation of what they believe was complicated grief with a partner. Switch roles. Have the pairs note what was similar and what was different about the two experiences of grief. Reform into the larger group. Have the pairs discuss their findings in the larger group.

Chapter One

Ambiguous Losses

An ambiguous loss may be defined in at least three different ways.

1. The loss is characterized by a lack of clarity or confusion surrounding the loss itself. There is no certainty of exactly *what* is happening, or *when* the uncertainty may end. Examples of this type of loss are hostages, MIAs and kidnappings. The events surrounding this type of loss are often unclear; the status and condition of the person is uncertain (dead or alive, harmed or unharmed); and the return of the person is hoped for, but unknown. Other examples of this type of loss include chronic illness, dementia, Alzheimer's disease, and coma. In these cases the grievers know that the person will die, but they are uncertain about *when* and *how*.

2. The event of the loss is clear, but the *perception* of the loss is unclear. The loss itself is clear, but the family[1] ignores the facts surrounding the loss event. The family may be unwilling to accept the loss, or may accept the loss too soon. One example of this is the physical absence of a person who remains psychologically present long after the person is clearly physically dead and buried or gone (divorce). Another example is a physically present person who is closed out of a family before he or she is dead (Alzheimer's disease, addiction, chronic illness, and coma).

3. The loss is unclear because it is not recognized, accepted, supported, validated, or ritualized by society. These types of losses have been renamed "disenfranchised losses" in the recent writings of Kenneth Doka,[2] and will be addressed in Chapter Two. Examples of this type of loss are prison, miscarriage, stillbirth, and abortion.

In all three types of ambiguous loss, there is no satisfactory *resolution* to the loss because of the ambiguity surrounding the loss or the perception of the loss, or the lack of recognition and support for the loss. Some ambiguous losses may fit one, two, or even all three categories.

Another way to understand ambiguous losses is to categorize them into *two* possibilities:[3]

1. the physical presence of the person/psychological absence

- Chronic illness
- dementia (Alzheimer's disease)
- coma
- addiction
- preoccupation with something or someone outside the family
- mental illness

2. the physical absence of the person/psychological presence

- hostage
- MIA
- missing child
- divorce

Naming a loss as ambiguous gives recognition to the fact that a loss has occurred and acknowledges that the ambiguity surrounding the loss may cause complications in the grieving process. Since one of the first tasks of grieving is to acknowledge that a loss has occurred, naming the loss is pivotal. Other tasks of grieving are to let go and reinvest in life—tasks that are extremely difficult in ambiguous losses.

Pauline Boss has done much of the research on ambiguous losses, particularly in relation to how *families* experience ambiguous losses.[4] According to Boss, the situation in families that results from the stress of ambiguous losses may be referred to as "boundary ambiguity" (*Ambiguous Loss* 165). Families are always trying to understand and maintain boundaries; this is very difficult, if not impossible, to do with ambiguous losses. Families may be unsure who is in and who is out of the system, and therefore be unable to reorganize themselves as a family. Although the *event* of the loss itself cannot be changed, it can be *clarified*. The *perception* of the loss can also be changed and clarified, thus clarifying who is in and who is out of the family system.

Given the challenge of acknowledging an ambiguous loss and agreeing on a common perception of the loss, what can pastoral ministers do to help families? Pastoral ministers must have an awareness of ambiguous loss in order to accurately *identify* this type of loss. According to Boss (168–169), we can also

- name the ambiguity as a stressor for families
- help provide an environment for family meetings to occur where all the various perceptions can be voiced and heard
- help provide information about the situation by helping to gather and clarify information surrounding the loss
- help provide the families with sources and choices for support besides one pastoral minister
- encourage and help provide families with a format to find meaning in loss

Pastoral ministers can be especially helpful with this last intervention. We can identify and call on various religious resources and help in facilitating appropriate rituals.

Some ambiguous losses will eventually reach a resolution—the MIA whose remains are found, the kidnapped child who is returned, or the person with Alzheimer's disease who dies. But the period of ambiguity may be a long one, and the loss may continue to be ambiguous if the family's perception continues to be that the person has not died. Some ambiguous losses will never have a clear resolution—the MIA or kidnapped child is never found, or the addicted person is continually in and out of recovery. Whether there is resolution or not, individuals and families will need help in learning to live with the uncertainty and will need encouragement and support in their grieving. Rituals will be important here, either in continuing the usual family rituals and finding a way to include the missing family member, or eventually, in ritualizing the death itself, when that finally becomes known or accepted (172).

Because of the difficulties in naming the loss, there are often interferences or difficulties in what Rando refers to as the first "R" process of mourning—recognizing the loss. This will often result in *absent* or *unanticipated grieving*. If grief appears to be absent, pastoral ministers may need to look at what is contributing to the absence of grief, in addition to the ambiguity of the loss itself. Factors such as dependency, fear of grieving, and guilt may be contributing to a reluctance to name and recognize the loss (*Grief, Dying and Death* 109). Because of the difficulties in resolving the loss, there are likely to be problems with the fourth and fifth "R" processes—relinquishing old attachments and readjusting to a new world. This may result in *chronic*, unending grieving. Again, factors other than the ambiguity of the loss may need to be explored: Is the relationship with the lost person overly dependent or irreplaceable? Is there any motivation to relinquish the ties? Or is the motivation to maintain the ties? Pastoral ministers may need to take an active role in assigning tasks to be completed in the grieving process (109–110). These tasks might include sorting through and giving away the deceased possessions, going through photographs, and writing to billing agencies and friends.

Alzheimer's Disease

Alzheimer's disease is a degenerative disease that is chronic, irreversible, and progressive. It attacks the brain and results in impairments in memory, thinking, and behavior. In defining Alzheimer's disease as an ambiguous loss, the emphasis is primarily on the loved ones surrounding the affected person. The person with Alzheimer's disease is, of course, also grieving as he or she experiences a variety of losses.

According to the three definitions of ambiguous loss given on page 13, Alzheimer's disease may be assessed as an ambiguous loss under either of the first two definitions: the loss is unclear or the perception of the loss is unclear, depending on the family's reactions and perceptions. Alzheimer's disease may also be categorized as an ambiguous loss under the two definitions given on page 14—a physically present, but (eventually) psychologically absent person. Naming the loss as ambiguous can help families and pastoral ministers to work through the loss more effectively.

Howard

Howard was sixty-six years old, one year into retirement, when his family began to notice that he was becoming forgetful. At first it was little things—forgetting to turn the heat down at night, or to lock the front door when he went out. Eventually the little things became bigger and of more concern—forgetting how to get home after driving somewhere, or forgetting to show up for a family get-together. Even as the number of incidents increased, most of the family was not worried. They attributed the forgetfulness to Howard's grief over the death of his beloved wife thirteen months before. Betty had kept track of most of these details for Howard. Then other changes began to appear. Howard, who was always gentle and accommodating, could now be strong-willed and stubborn.

Howard had three grown children—two married sons, John (45) and Jeff (43), and a single daughter, Jill (38)—who all lived nearby. His daughter was concerned about Howard's forgetfulness and suggested that he see a doctor. But Howard hadn't been to a doctor since his family physician had retired ten years earlier. "I never missed a day of work in my life," he bragged, "except for Mom's funeral. I feel fine." Jill remained concerned and began checking on him on a daily basis. Although her two brothers did not share in her concern, they agreed to keep an eye on Dad.

One day Howard could not be found anywhere. After checking at his home and the Senior Center and with all of his friends, his daughter became worried. Her brothers joined her in the search. When night came and Dad was still nowhere to be found, they called the police. The next day they received a call from the police. Howard had been located at a restaurant a few hours away. He was confused and disoriented, but he knew his name and said he wanted to go home.

After this incident the family was able to convince Howard to go to the doctor—just for a checkup. Some of them now began to fear the worst, yet were unsure what the worst would be. Others remained sure everything would be all right. The diagnosis was Alzheimer's disease. The doctor suggested that the family meet with a counselor or minister to sort out what this meant and how they would support and care for Howard in the days ahead.

There are a number of issues that need to be acknowledged and addressed here so that grieving can proceed. This case will continue to be explored from the perspective of the pastoral minister[5] who is called in to help the family sort out what is going on and to help them in their grieving.

Rose, a pastoral associate at Howard's church, is called in to talk with the family. Before she meets with them, she lays out a genogram[6] of what she knows of the makeup of the family.

Rose asks to meet with all of the family members, including the four grandchildren. To prepare for this meeting, she reviews what she knows about Alzheimer's disease, particularly as an ambiguous loss. Rose is aware that she is being asked to come into the picture early on in the grieving process. Most of the family may still be in *shock* or *denial* over the diagnosis. Her primary role is to *listen* as she encourages the family to express all their feelings—whatever they may be, and however different. She will need to let them know that what they are experiencing is normal and part of the *beginning* of a *grieving process*.

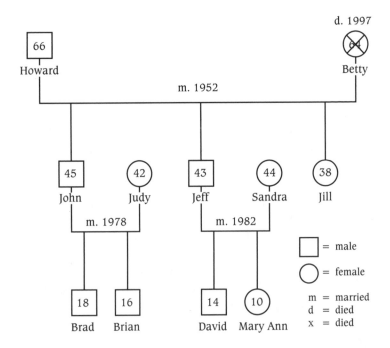

Rose can also help the family as they *gather* and try to understand *information* about Alzheimer's disease, including treatment and caregiving. She realizes that this may be the start of a very long process and that she needs to be with the family where they are now, even if that is in denial. She needs to be *patient, calm, nonjudgmental,* and *compassionate.* She realizes that not only is this family in the first phase of grief, they are in the *first stage* of *caregiving bereavement*—the stage that occurs *during caregiving.* This stage begins with the diagnosis itself and proceeds through deterioration that evokes feelings of powerlessness and loss, when an "empty space" emerges and the caregivers start their long process of detachment. They are at the very beginning of what may be a long, agonizing process. They may feel disoriented and bewildered as each family member struggles to come to terms with a diagnosis that brings an unknown future. The *second stage* of *caregiver bereavement* will occur *after Howard's physical death,* when grief becomes acute and the empty space enlarges. Caregivers try to fill the empty space as they begin to reconstruct their lives and get on with life without caregiving and without their loved one. Eventually they will experience both relief and recovery (Jones and Martinson 175).

Part of Rose's first conversation with the family is printed here (see the genogram on page 18 for identifying data).

Rose: Thank you for inviting me here today. It is a privilege for me to be with you as you gather together as a family to talk about Howard's diagnosis and what this means to you as a family. I see my role here today as listener and facilitator. Everyone's voice is important and I will be asking each one of you for input. Here are the ground rules as I see them:

Each person will have an opportunity to speak, but no one *has* to speak. You have the right to pass.

No one person or opinion is right or wrong. We are here to *listen* to each other so that we can better understand where we are coming from as individuals and as a family. We are not here to convince each other of our views.

We are here because of our love for Howard and our concern for his well-being and future care. *Any* feeling we have is acceptable because we know it originates in our love for Howard.

How does that sound?

19

Jill: Let's get started! Even though we all don't go to church, we agreed it would be good for you to start with a prayer.

Rose: I'd like that. I'll start. Please join in wherever you like.

Loving God, we are gathered here today—as a family—to talk about our father and grandfather, Howard Jones. Be with us in our conversation as we try to understand and express what is in our hearts. Help us to be patient with each other and to have the courage to say what we are really feeling.

Each of us has special needs that we bring here today, and I now invite any who would like to mention what that need is. I'll start. I need to be able to hear each of you—wherever you may be. I pray for guidance in listening.

Jill: I tend to talk too much. I pray that I can keep quiet so that others can talk.

John: I pray for a cure so that we don't have to deal with this.

Brad: I pray that Grandpa will be here to see me graduate from high school *and* college.

Judy: I don't know what to pray, but I'm glad we're praying as a family.

(silence)

Rose: Anyone else?

Sandra: I need to have some answers. I pray that I can get some today.

(silence)

Rose: Dear God, we gather these hopes and needs—those we have just expressed and those that remain in our hearts, and give them over to you. We ask your blessing on all that we say and do today. In Christ's name we pray. Amen.

There are nine family members gathered here today. I'd like to give everyone a chance to speak at least once. Who would like to start?

Jill: I know I said I needed to be quiet so others could talk, but that will be easier for me after I say what I want to say. I just want to say that I can't believe that I was the only one who saw what was happening with Dad and how sick he was. I can't help but think that if we had only got him to a doctor sooner …

Jeff (interrupting): There you go again, Jill. You always think only you know what is best. You know the doctor said that wouldn't have helped.

John: Yeah. And I'm still not sure that Dad is really as sick as you think he is.

Rose: Jill, Jeff, and John, you are all speaking what is in your hearts, and this is good. I wonder if it would be helpful if I kept track of some of the issues and feelings that you are expressing. (Writes on newsprint: Issues/Feelings.)

Rose (writing): Issue Number 1: Need to understand more about Alzheimer's disease.

Rose: Along with this issue, could you also identify a feeling that you are having?

Jill and Jeff: Anger.

Rose (writing): Feeling Number 1: Anger.

Rose: We'll come back to that. Let's see if anyone else wants to say what they are feeling ...

Rose's purpose is to encourage the family to express their feelings and concerns without having the meeting turn into a blaming session. Doing this means that she will take an active role in keeping the family discussion both open and focused. She needs to affirm, summarize, and draw out emotions. She continues to encourage each person to speak and to keep track of what is being said. She does not add her own opinion or perspective but focuses on understanding and summarizing the various perspectives of the people gathered. At the end of the session Rose has sheets full of emotions and issues. She works with the family to prioritize the issues and helps identify resources: where to get information on Alzheimer's disease, what support groups exist, and (for those who asked) what religious resources may be helpful (such as particular Scripture passages and prayers). Rose assures them that she will be a supportive presence throughout Howard's illness. She also reminds them that she is not a professional counselor, and there may come a time when some or all of them will desire professional counseling and she will help in that referral.[7]

Rose is called on a number of times throughout Howard's seven-year illness, and remains a supportive, pastoral presence in the family. Her ministry includes the following:

Naming the Beast — helping the family to name and understand Alzheimer's disease as an ambiguous loss

Taming the Beast

- *Using empathy*[8]— working with the family to understand their perspective of Howard's illness

21

- *Gathering information* — empowering the family to gather as much information as is needed
- *Widening the circle of care* — encouraging a broad range of resources, including the parish community
- *Providing a continual pastoral presence* — as a minister and as a community of faith, including Howard and his family in:
  - community prayers
  - pastoral visitation to the homebound
  - greeting cards and notes of support and encouragement
  - special blessings of those who are ill and their caregivers
  - church bulletins and newsletters
  - rituals for those experiencing loss

Renaming the Beast or dealing with questions of faith — being willing to respond to the thornier theological and moral issues that arise: Why did God do this to Dad? Why doesn't he die? Why does he have to suffer so long? If he stops eating, should we have a feeding tube inserted?

Rose's ministry and the ministry of the worshiping community continued on after Howard's death in many of the same ways. However, much of the grieving and ministry with the person with Alzheimer's disease occurs *before* death, in the caregiving period. This unique situation presents caregivers and pastoral ministers with special challenges, some of which have already been noted. Other challenges include:

- the continual change in roles experienced by the person with Alzheimer's disease and the family
- the refusal of the affected person and the family to name and acknowledge the losses that continue to occur
- the long-term uncertainty and ambiguity surrounding the progression of the disease
- the amounts of physical, emotional, and spiritual strain on the caregivers and pastoral ministers
- the long-term nature of anticipatory grieving

- the tendency to prematurely detach

These last two points require particular attention.

Anticipatory Grief and Premature Detachment

Anticipatory grief is grief that is experienced *before* an actual loss occurs. In this case, it is the grief that is experienced *before* Howard dies. The term was actually coined during World War II by Erich Lindemann, who used the phrase to describe a situation in which a soldier had returned home after being away a long time to find that his wife was no longer in love with him and wanted a divorce. According to Lindemann, the wife had mourned her husband's absence and had detached herself from him, in anticipation of his not returning. In this case, there was no actual death, but the threat of a death. We may also experience anticipatory loss in relation to the potential loss of social roles (retirement), bodily functions (aging), or a loved possession (selling a home).

In Howard's case, he and his family experienced anticipatory loss in relation to his future death, and to his ongoing losses in role, functioning, and the ability to relate. For Howard's loved ones, anticipatory grief was the grief they experienced in the caregiving stage of their bereavement. As Howard became more forgetful, less independent, less communicative, and in need of more care, both he and his family continued to experience anticipatory grief. They grieved

- the loss of life as they had known it—the *past*
- the ongoing and continuing losses—the *present*
- and the loss of life as they had envisioned it happening—the *future*[9]

Understanding that what they were experiencing had a name—*anticipatory grief*—was extremely helpful. Learning that it also had a purpose, and an end, helped Howard's family to feel less anxious and more hopeful. Knowing that with anticipatory grief there is more ambivalence and more denial (Rando, "Anticipatory Grief" 9) enabled them to be less ashamed of their feelings. As their experience of grief seemed to be increasing with time, they began to worry if they would make it through. They also worried what they would do when

Howard died. It was a relief for them to learn that a characteristic of anticipatory grief is that it accelerates as death nears, but ends with death as *post-death grief* appears. Post-death grief would actually decrease with time, making the most painful time of grieving for them the time they were currently living through (10).

It was also helpful to understand that part of the stress that they were experiencing was because of the *length* of Howard's illness. Studies indicate that as the length of an illness progresses beyond eighteen months, there is a higher rate of post-death anger and an increase in complicated (abnormal) grief (20). It was also helpful to learn that anticipatory grief had its own stages that they could relate to (Spiegel):

- shock
- attempts at control — busyness
- regression — dealing with loss from what was done in the past
- adaptive stage — being ready to face a reintegration with self and others

As helpful as this was, Howard's family realized that there were at least two obstacles in anticipatory grief:

1. Experiencing the losses is not the same as grieving the losses; anticipatory grieving requires hard, continuous *work* over a long time.

2. Because of the length of the illness and grieving, there is a tendency in anticipatory grieving for families to *prematurely detach* from their loved one, who is still alive.

Three years into Howard's illness he no longer recognized members of his family. He required around-the-clock care to attend to his physical needs and to maintain his safety. By this time all the members of the family had come to terms with the seriousness of Howard's illness and the eventual outcome of death. His grandsons—Brad (21), Brian (19), and David (17)—were having a difficult time keeping up a relationship with Grandpa. They dreaded their visits with him when they tried to tell him what was going on in their lives only to find that he didn't even know who they were. They began to plan events to get out of visiting him, and they no longer talked about having Grandpa at their activities. One day Jill overheard David telling a friend that his grandfather was dead. Jill was outraged and confronted David. He responded, "I know he's not dead, but it's like he is. I no longer have the Grandpa I had. He's not a part of my life. He doesn't even know I exist. He might as well be dead."

David (and Brad and Brian) are detaching from their grandfather. Although this is normal and to be expected, it will be unfortunate if they continue to do this while Howard is still alive. Although he can no longer relate to them as before, he still needs to be related to. David, Brad, and Brian need to find new ways to grieve the loss of the grandfather they knew while continuing to relate to the grandfather they now have. They will need their family's help and Rose's to learn how to do this.

Once again, Rose's unique role as pastoral minister was of special help to them in their anticipatory grieving. She was able to bring to the foreground the broader questions of meaning and faith and the value of life, when they got caught up in how things used to be. She was able to work with them to ritualize the passing of certain events in their lives and to include Grandpa in new ways in these rituals. She was able to be present to them in their anger and detachment and to represent and remind them of God's love and concern for them. Rose was also their link to a community of faith that supported them and held them in their care.

Divorce

Jim and Terry had been married for twelve years and were the parents of two children, Mindy (10) and Michael (8). They had been having trouble in their marriage for a number of years. After six months of marriage counseling they decided to separate. They agreed that it was best for the children to stay at the house with Terry. Jim moved into a small apartment. Since they were still unsure about divorce, they decided on a trial separation of six months. During this time the children stayed with Terry from Monday to Friday and spent every other weekend with Jim. During the week Jim was over at least two to three evenings to help with homework, baby-sit if Terry had to go out, or attend school and sports functions with the kids. Except for every other weekend with only Dad, Mindy and Michael's life changed very little. They actually saw more of Dad now than they ever had before. They were a bit confused about their mother's tears and constant talk about Dad being gone.

At the end of six months, Terry was ready to have Jim move back in and try to work on the marriage. She had seen the separation as temporary, a time apart so they could come back together. Jim, however, liked the new arrangement and wanted to proceed with a legal separation and divorce.

Terry talked about Jim all the time, even though he came over less often during the week and preferred seeing the children without Terry being there. Jim also started dating, which upset Terry. One day in religion class Mindy was sharing that she had two homes. When one of the other children asked if her parents were divorced Mindy replied, "Oh, no—at least I don't think so. Mom still sets Dad's place at dinner every night, and Dad's tools are still in the garage."

This situation represents another type of ambiguous loss—a physical absence, but psychological presence. The children are not sure whether Dad is in or out of the family system, and Terry adds to the confusion by setting Jim's place at dinner and talking about his return. This is a critical and very difficult time in the grieving process—a time when only Jim seems ready to acknowledge that separation and loss have occurred. Mindy and Michael are caught between Dad talking about a future *without* Mom and Mom talking about a future *with* Dad. Even in this confusion and ambiguity, grieving can and actually *needs* to begin.

At the very least, the family can name the ambiguity of the loss and the differing perceptions and expectations surrounding that ambiguity. They can also name what they have lost:

- what *was* — being together as a family, doing things with all four members of the family
- what *is* — Dad's absence during the week—at meals, at bedtime, and at homework; weekends at their own house
- what *would have been* — a sense of security about the future as a family; holidays as they have always known them

  Terry and Jim could add to this list:

- companionship

- income
- parenting as a couple
- someone to argue with
- someone to share household chores with

The future will probably continue to hold additional losses, whether Jim and Terry divorce or reconcile. But it is the present losses that need clarification and a discussion of the differences in perceptions and hopes for the future. Naming the ambiguity of the loss (separation), listing other concrete losses, and expressing differing perceptions and hopes will help give the family some clarity to their grief and initial permission to grieve the losses that are occurring. Since Terry is trying to deny or downplay much of the actual loss of the separation, this process may be most difficult for her, but it is necessary for the health and well-being of the family.

One year later Terry and Jim do divorce. Terry no longer sets a place for Jim and his tools (and other items) have all been moved out. The loss seems less ambiguous and more definite, but certainly still painful. The children continue to talk about Dad almost every day and Terry continues to talk about the way life used to be before the divorce, remembering mostly the good times. She says such things as, "Remember how much fun we had when we all went camping?"

Though now definitely, physically absent from the home, Jim remains a strong psychological presence. When Mindy is asked about her parents she reports," Oh yeah, they're divorced, but I think they'll be getting back together sometime soon."

The loss remains ambiguous and the grieving remains complicated. Certain factors continue to enhance complications in grieving, but other factors help the family in their grief. Frank, the deacon at their church, sits down with Terry—at her request—to help her list what is helping and what continues to hinder her in her grieving.

What Is Helping

1. Good social and faith resources, lots of friends and a supportive church community

2. A supportive and open family (Mom and Dad) who can talk about the divorce without blaming each other

3. A stable financial situation

4. Children who are not taking sides

What Is Hurting

1. Ambiguity of the loss

2. Other losses (secondary losses[10]):

   - of self-esteem
   - of identity
   - of belief that marriage is forever
   - of co-parent, mechanic, chauffeur, gardener, friend, companion, and lover

3. Unresolved anger in marriage relationship (intense feelings)

4. Belief that divorce was preventable

Terry was also able to see that a number of potentially complicating factors were *not* present:

- The children were not so young they couldn't understand.
- There were no other major stressors or losses in the family.
- The family system was not inflexible or condemning.
- There was no known generational legacy of unresolved loss.

Terry realized that although the loss was complicated, there were a number of factors present that could help her in her grieving. Terry was also able to see how she contributed to the ambiguity of the loss, and therefore the complications, by her constant talk about what was and what might be. She began to limit her talk about a glorified past and her hopes for a reconciled future—at least in front of the children.

As the ambiguity became less dominant, the loss became clearer and the children were able to talk more about their own hopes and fears and to grieve the loss of life as they had known it and as they had imagined it would always be. In doing so, they could more honestly see that their new life had some disadvantages, but it also had some advantages—less fighting, more one-on-one time with Dad, and a new calmness in family outings.

Resourcing the Spiritual

For Terry, Jim, Mindy, and Michael Peters it was important to some-how *ritualize* the changes that had occurred in their family. They be-lieved that doing so would help them let go of the past and look forward to the future with a new sense of hope. Frank (their deacon) explained some possible reasons for enacting a ritual—to help with and symbolize understanding, forgiveness, transition, healing, or meaning. He also talked about the difference between a *mythic ritual* that conveys the sense that everything is going to be all right; and a *parabolic ritual* that embraces the discordant and admits the pain (Anderson and Foley 33). This second type of ritual—the para-bolic—may be especially effective in ambiguous losses like divorce, and it was this type of ritual that the Peters family chose.

Pastoral ministers of any denomination can work with divorcing families to come up with rituals that will help in the transition, the healing, and the search for meaning in their grieving. The rituals may be simple and nonreligious—lighting a candle, or planting a tree—or more elaborate and more overtly religious—doing services of hope and healing, or writing or reciting prayers of lament.[11] The Peters fam-ily devised a simple ritual of letting go in which each family member wrote down on a piece of paper what was most painful in the divorce. They then shared this hurt with everyone in the family. Each person was invited to let go of that hurt in whatever way was appropriate for them. Michael chose to place his hurts in a balloon, blow it up, and watch it drift away. Mindy chose to throw hers in a river and watch it float away. Jim chose to rip his up and to bury the pieces. Terry had the most trouble letting go of the hurt and asked to keep hers in her jewelry box. With Frank's encouragement, she was able to decorate her hurt, so although she could not let it go, she could see that it was being transformed. Terry, Jim, Mindy, and Michael ended their ritual with Frank leading them in a prayer for healing, health, and growth. They also planted two new trees at their separate homes, symbolizing the hope for new life and new growth.

Study Questions

1. What is an ambiguous loss? In what three ways can it be defined?
2. Name three things a pastoral minister can do to help families experiencing ambiguous loss.
3. What type of unresolved grief is associated with ambiguous loss? What factors may be contributing to the ambiguity?
4. What are the two stages of caregiving bereavement?
5. What are some of the particular challenges for the family of a person with Alzheimer's disease?
6. What is anticipatory grief? What are its three foci? What are its stages? How do anticipatory grief and premature detachment contribute to complicated grief for the family of a person with Alzheimer's disease?
7. What are some of the secondary losses involved in divorce?

Practicums

1. Break up the larger group into groups of three to four. Have each small group develop a ritual for Howard's family (Alzheimer's disease case) or for the Peters family (divorce).
2. Have the small groups (three to four) discuss how they would respond to the following questions that Howard's family raised.
   - Why did God do this to Dad? Grandpa?
   - Why does he have to suffer so much?
   - Should we have a feeding tube inserted if he stops eating?
3. Have one person take the role of one member of Howard's family who is struggling with one of these questions. Have another person play pastoral minister. Let the two talk for a few minutes. (The other two persons should serve as silent observers.) After ten minutes have the observers give feedback.
   - What issues emerged?
   - What was most difficult? Why?

- What was most helpful? Why?
- What skills were used? (See the Appendix.)

In giving feedback make sure the observers focus on strengths, and also comment on what was missing. Give the persons in the role-play sufficient time to debrief.

Chapter Two

Disenfranchised Losses

The common term used to describe the grief that occurs when a loss is not recognized by society is "disenfranchised grief." Disenfranchised grief is also known as stigmatized or unsanctioned loss, and hidden sorrow. Kenneth Doka ("Recognizing Hidden Sorrow" 272–274) has defined disenfranchised grief as grief that is experienced when a loss cannot be "openly acknowledged, publicly named, or socially supported."

Grief is described as "disenfranchised" if any of the following characteristics are present:

- **The relationship with the deceased is not recognized.**
  Relationships that are not recognized include those that are not recognized by kinship (foster parents, counselors, co-workers, friends, and neighbors), as well as those not publicly recognized or socially sanctioned (extramarital affairs, homosexual relationships, and past relationships). As a former lover or a former daughter-in-law, we are not seen as primary grievers and are not granted the status of the present daughter-in-law, or the present lover, regardless of the quality of the relationship. As gay partners who are part of present relationships, we are often not accepted as kin or as having the same legal right as heterosexual spouses. There is an implicit assumption that being related to someone or legally married to someone means that we are *close* to that person. There is also the assumption that being close to someone is immaterial, and that it is our kinship with them that "counts" in "grieving rights."[1]

- **The loss is not recognized.**
  Losses in this category include those that society does not designate as *significant*—as deserving the full "gamut of grief."[2] Prenatal deaths, miscarriages, stillbirths, and abortions are categorized here. Other losses that may not be recognized are the

social deaths that occur when our loved one is institutionalized, when a mother gives her child for adoption or foster care, or when our loved one has been declared brain-dead but is still biologically alive. "Grieving rules"—rules that name who, what, when, where, how, how long, and for whom we should grieve—dictate that the loss cannot be fully recognized because no actual death has occurred.

- **The griever is not recognized.**
The loss *is* recognized, but the griever is not. The griever is seen as not capable of grieving—too young, too old, mentally ill. People in these categories are often excluded from funerals and from post-death grief talk.

Disenfranchised grievers fall outside the "grieving rules" set by a specific society. These rules define *who* has a "legitimate" right to grieve as well as what *losses* are recognized and sanctioned.

In all these cases there is grief that cannot be fully expressed, accepted, and sanctioned. Disenfranchised grief is complicated grief for the following reasons:

- Feelings of anger, guilt, and powerlessness are increased, leading to complications in grieving.

- Ambivalent relationships and concurrent crises and stressors are likely to be present, which can cause complications in the grieving. For instance, ambivalent relationships are likely to be present in cases of abortion, and Alzheimer's disease, and between ex-spouses and lovers. Concurrent stressors and crises that are likely to be present include legal and inheritance problems in nontraditional relationships (gay or cohabiting relationships).

- Factors that normally facilitate grieving are not present, such as participation in the funeral rites. When we as grievers are not recognized or not seen as capable of grief, we are unlikely to be included in grieving rituals.

- The very nature of disenfranchised grief precludes support because there is no recognized public role afforded to disenfranchised grievers, as is the case in an extramarital affair, or the woman who has had an abortion.

In Chapter One Alzheimer's disease was described as an ambiguous loss. It may also fit the category of disenfranchised grief when the griever's relationship is not recognized, when the griever is not recognized, or when the losses surrounding Alzheimer's disease are not recognized. In Howard's case (page 17), his friends are potentially disenfranchised grievers because they are not recognized by significant kin relationship and are not seen as capable of grief (too old). Howard's younger grandchildren could also fall into this category (too young). The many losses Howard and his family and friends go through may also not be considered significant (by grieving rules standards) until he actually dies.

Chapter One also listed three possibilities that define a loss as ambiguous (page 13). Only one of those possibilities needs to exist to categorize a loss as ambiguous. Alzheimer's disease may fit all three definitions:

1. There is lack of certainty surrounding the progression of the illness and the time and manner of death.

2. The affected person remains physically present but psychologically absent and is closed out of the family before his or her death.

3. The losses occurring in the progression of the illness are not supported and validated by society as legitimate.

Alzheimer's disease is a particularly complicated loss because it is both an ambiguous loss *and* a disenfranchised loss. This chapter focuses on three more types of disenfranchised losses: suicide, AIDS, and abortion.

Suicide

There is little dispute in the literature that suicide is one of the most difficult deaths survivors must deal with (Rando, *Complicated Mourning* 523). Reasons for this include the lack of anticipation, the untimeliness of the death, the belief that the death was preventable, and the often-violent means of death (524).

Suicide, along with AIDS, carries a strong social and moral "stigma"—an accompanying judgment on the manner of death and the life of the person who dies. Survivors of suicide[3] are often reluctant to reveal that the death of their loved one was a suicide for a number of reasons (Rando, *Complicated Mourning* 531; Parsons 648):

- Suicide survivors are viewed more negatively than are other survivors; more blame is placed on them for the death.

- Suicide survivors fear the legal, moral, and financial repercussions of a suicide—withholding life insurance payments, associating suicide with a crime or with an unpardonable sin.

- Suicide survivors often have an enormous amount of guilt and shame surrounding the suicide. They may believe that they could have prevented the suicide.

- Suicide survivors are fearful of their own self-destructive thoughts and behaviors that are common after a suicide.

- Suicide survivors perceive that if the death is a suicide they will not receive the same sort of social support as a nonsuicidal death.

- Suicide survivors feel responsible for making sense of the death and for answering why the loved ones took their own life. This is a question that survivors cannot answer.

Being a socially unsanctioned death with a stigma is sufficient to classify suicide as a complicated loss. Suicide has three additional complicating factors: it is *sudden*, *traumatic*, and usually *violent*.

Sharon

Sharon came home from work one night and found the front door unlocked. Since Gary's car was in the driveway, she thought he must have arrived home early for a change. She walked into the house heading for the kitchen and a cup of coffee before starting dinner. She called out to Gary, but got no reply, then realized that the shower was going. She sat down with her coffee and took a quick look at the paper before starting dinner. After twenty or thirty minutes, she realized that the shower was still going. She once more called out to Gary, but got no reply. She finished cutting the vegetables then walked upstairs to see why he was in the shower so long. She opened the bathroom door and called his name. No reply. Only then did Sharon begin to worry, "Maybe he fell and hit his head." She ran over to the shower stall and pulled open the curtain, half-expecting Gary to jump out and scare her, or to pull her in the shower with him. Nothing in her life up to this point had prepared her for what she saw next. Gary was sitting on the shower floor, fully clothed, with the shower streaming down on him. He held a gun in his hand and parts of his head were splattered all over the shower stall. The floor of the stall was red and Sharon realized it was Gary's blood. She doesn't remember exactly what happened next. Only blackness, then sirens and waking up in a hospital emergency room with a police officer by her side.

She has never been able to remember what happened after seeing Gary's body. She is told that she called 911; when the paramedics arrived they found her slumped in the shower next to Gary, with blood all over her. The police thought she had killed Gary. Only after an autopsy and investigation was she cleared.

Sometimes Sharon thought it would have made things easier if she *had* been the one who killed Gary—at least she would have known why he died. Their marriage had been troubled for many years and they had recently talked about divorce. In the last few weeks Gary had seemed to accept the end of the marriage and was finally able to talk of a future without Sharon. Now Sharon was left with questions: Why did Gary kill himself after seeming to come to terms with life? Was it her fault? Would he have done this if she hadn't pushed for divorce? Would she have been able to stop him if she had come home earlier that night? Why did he do this to her? Was it his way of getting revenge? She had so many questions and so much guilt.

Two years after Gary's death Sharon is still haunted by unanswered questions. She sells the house, moves to another town, and changes jobs. She keeps her past life a secret, telling others only that she is widowed. She never discloses the circumstances surrounding Gary's death.

In a search for meaning in her life and forgiveness for what she sees as her part in Gary's death, Sharon begins to attend church services. She reads in the church bulletin that there is a church support group for widows. She decides to go and see if anyone has a story anything like hers. She is reluctant and ashamed but tired of feeling so alone. She attends a number of meetings without sharing her story. After one meeting she asks to meet with the facilitator of the group. Sharon tells her she is afraid to share her story with the group and wants to try it out on her first.

Given all the complications surrounding Gary's death, the grief group facilitator may feel overwhelmed. She is grateful that she is familiar with suicidal grief and that she has already had to examine her own feelings and beliefs when she was asked to do a memorial service for a teenager who had committed suicide.

Just as Alzheimer's grief has particular "stages," so too does suicidal grief. Basically, suicidal grief follows the stages of "ordinary" grief, but with additional tasks and difficulties (Parsons 647–651):

- **Shock and Denial**[4]
  The suicidal death is *sudden* and often *violent*. Survivors must work through denial by accepting that a death has occurred *and* that the death was a suicide. Denial is a necessary and protective defense, but it must give way to the reality of the loss. This is particularly difficult in suicidal grief because survivors often conceal the fact that a loved one's death was a suicide. Failure to acknowledge that the death was a suicide *halts* the grieving process.

- **Yearning and Protest**
  Suicide survivors are often not encouraged to express emotions, particularly because emotions are usually *intense* feelings of anger, guilt, and relief. When these feelings are denied, they are suppressed and become directed inwardly or outwardly. When directed inwardly, these feelings may lead to obsessive thoughts about the survivor's role in a loved one's death, and to self-destructive behavior. When directed outwardly, survivors may inappropriately project anger or guilt onto another person, agency, or institution. Survivors of suicide are prevented from checking with reality (that the death was a suicide and that the feelings experienced are intense). A complicit conspiracy of silence is maintained. Grieving is *distorted*.

- **Disorganization**
  For survivors of suicide, feelings of self-pity, depression, and hopelessness are complicated by a perceived and actual lack of

support. The secretiveness and the stigma of suicide make grieving very difficult. Grief can become *chronic*.

Because of these additional factors at each stage of grief, it is very difficult to get to the fourth and final stage of grief—Reorganization. Survivors of suicide are prone to numerous complications in grieving at every "R" process, and are thus liable to potentially experience every type of unresolved grief—absent, inhibited, conflicted (distorted), chronic, unanticipated, and abbreviated.

Survivors of suicide will also have a tendency to (Parsons 650–654):

- re-engage in relationships as quickly as possible, often with a person who needs nurturance (someone who is chronically ill or who has a disability)

- plan to save the world by investing energies in activities such as a crusade to end world hunger

- become openly self-destructive, including having thoughts of taking their own life (suicidal ideation)

- use new intimate relationships to act out grievances against the deceased loved one

- become attracted to persons who are suicidal, perhaps trying to stop a suicide from happening again

What Can We As Survivors Do?

- Come to terms with the reality of the death as a suicide; don't get stuck in denial.

- Know that we are not alone in our experience or in our grief; join a support group for survivors of suicide. Read and learn about other survivors of suicide.

- Learn to identify and express all feelings, especially "negative" ones.[5] Talk to friends, counselors, ministers, and God. Learn to yell, scream, and cry and to verbalize all feelings. Write letters to the deceased or to God. Keep a journal of feelings and questions.

- Seek help with theological questions: Why did God do this? Where is God in our suffering? Does God forgive those who take their own lives? Can we forgive our loved one? Does God forgive us?

- Keep healthy through physical exercise, good nutrition, enjoyable activities, prayer, and meditation. Refrain from depressants, alcohol, and other drugs.

- Learn to accept that some questions may never be answered. Learn to be patient with the grieving process and with ourselves. Gain strength from being survivors, not victims.[6]

What Can Pastoral Ministers Do?

- Learn all we can about suicide—reasons, signs, interventions, and resources. Read, take workshops, and talk to professionals.

- Spend time with our own grief. Learn how to become "good" grievers by doing our own current and unfinished grief work.

- Be nonjudgmental, supportive, and caring with survivors. Help survivors to deal with the death being a suicide.

- Watch for signs of complicated grieving, particularly excessive anger and excessive guilt, which are signs of conflicted or distorted grief.

- Become familiar with what our own denominational tradition has said about suicide.[7]

- Assist survivors to overcome self-admonitions about grieving and to work at changing and removing subtle forces in the church and society that repress and prevent the open expression of grief following a suicide.

- Intervene early in survivor grief. Be available. Encourage communication. Be supportive, gentle, and understanding. Listen. Help survivors to move out of denial.

- Encourage movement through anger, guilt, and shame. Allow the expression of *all* feelings. Allow survivors to express anger at God. Address the suicide openly. Address and confront depression, irrational beliefs, and hopelessness.

- Recognize and address specific pastoral/theological issues, such as
  - anxiety and confusion about damnation and salvation
  - assurance of forgiveness

- need for the topic of suicide to be addressed through homilies, lectures, presentations, and workshops
- help in praying, planning funerals, memorial services, and appropriate rituals

Prayer may take the form of lament (see endnote 11, page 121). "Theologically, [lament] is based on a belief that God will hear and must hear because it is the business of God to hear; psychologically [lament] is based on a belief that suffering people will not get help if they keep quiet" (Karaban, "Pastoral Implications" 30).

Rituals for survivors may include:

- writing a letter to the deceased and bringing it to the cemetery (or place where cremains are kept) and reading it out loud, or burning it and burying the ashes

- drawing a picture of our experience of grief and loss and sharing it with a counselor, minister, friend, or family member (See the Appendix.)

- symbolizing the ending of earthly life and the beginning of life eternal by burying a symbol in the ground and lighting a candle, or by planting a tree

- putting together a scrapbook of the deceased's life so that we remember the whole life, not just how they died

- donating to a life-giving charity in the deceased's name, helping feed the homeless on the death anniversary, or starting a scholarship in the deceased's name

- creating or participating in rituals of healing and forgiveness sponsored by our faith community

• Become familiar with religious resources and rituals surrounding suicide. Know what Scripture says about suicide.[8] There are actually very few places where suicide is mentioned in Scripture. There is simply a report of what happened; no judgment is made about the action. In Scripture, suicide or attempted suicide is reported eleven times:

Old Testament:

1. Saul falls upon his own sword (1 Sm 31:4); assisted suicide, Saul is slain at his own request by an Amalekite (2 Sm 1:1–16).

2. Saul's armor bearer falls on his own sword (1 Sm 31:5).

3. Samson causes a building to fall on him (Jgs 16:28–31).

4. Ahithophel hangs himself (2 Sm 17:23).

5. Abimelech, assisted suicide, armor bearer kills him upon his request (Jgs 9:52–54).

6. Zimri burns down the king's house while he is inside (1 Kgs 16:18–19).

7. Jonah attempts suicide (Jon 1–4).[9]

Apocrypha:

8. Eleazar gives his life in battle, elephant falls upon him (1 Mc 6:43–47).

9. Razis (2 Mc 14:41–46) falls on his own sword.

New Testament:

10. Judas hangs himself (Mt 27:3–5; Acts 1:18).

11. Philippian jailer attempts to kill himself with his sword (Acts 16:27–28).

These passages alone are not sufficient to understand how Judaism, Christianity, or the churches have viewed suicide. Other scriptural passages[10] that need to be considered include the following:

• passages that condemn the taking of life as a violation of God's creation (such as Gn 1:1–2,4a, 2:4b–25 and Eccl 3:1–3)

• passages that condemn the taking of life as a violation of God's commandment (such as Ex 20:13, Dt 4:9, 5:17, Rv 2:10–11)

• passages that pardon sinful acts because God is a loving and forgiving God (Mt 12:31, Mk 3:28–30, Lk 12:10, and Rom 8:1–2,10–11,38–39)

Grief ministers, like survivors, need to realize that we are not alone in this. The whole community of faith is responsible for comforting the grieving. The community can join together to:

- become a caring church that is committed to (1) *prevention* before suicide, by promoting emotional well-being through education; (2) *intervention* during suicide, by actively ministering to those who are suicidal; and (3) *postvention* after suicide, by actively ministering to those who are survivors of suicide.[11]

- become proactive in our ministry by learning and teaching about suicide *before* being faced with a tragic suicide.

- develop rituals of letting go, forgiving, and healing that can be used with survivors of suicide.

- understand the church's history and position on suicide by looking at Scripture and church teachings.

AIDS

Persons with AIDS (PWA[12]) and their survivors are at significant risk for complicated grieving for the following reasons:

- AIDS is a lengthy and unpredictable illness.

- Even though AIDS is a lengthy illness, death may occur suddenly.

- PWA or survivors may perceive that the illness was preventable.

- PWA and survivors may lack social support.

- Survivors may experience multiple deaths from AIDS, particularly in the gay community.

- PWA have a high potential for suicide.

Unique issues for PWA and their caregivers include stigmatization, discrimination, problems obtaining health care, fear of infection, cruelty, lack of support, a feeling of victimization, seeing the illness as a punishment, helplessness, hopelessness, excessive denial, excessive guilt, and anger toward self, God, or the medical community. AIDS-related deaths are particularly difficult for caregivers and survivors because these deaths force us to come to terms with our own personal mortality (Smith 690). PWA are at high risk for suicide. They are sixty-six times more likely to commit suicide than someone in the general population (Christensen 142).

Ministering to PWA and their families presents a number of challenges to pastoral ministers. As in any crisis situation, PWA and their caregivers and loved ones are faced with challenges and opportunities, as can be seen in the following case.

Anthony

Anthony had been doing drugs since he was nineteen. He started with pot and worked his way up to cocaine. He had been in rehab treatment programs twice before and had twice gone back to using. At thirty, he was ready to try again. He was dating Luisa, who was not into drugs and who told Anthony he must be off drugs before they could consider marriage. Anthony entered treatment again and stayed clean for two years. He and Luisa were married and Luisa was expecting their first child. Lately Anthony was experiencing some health problems, and at Luisa's insistence, went for a checkup. In taking his medical history the doctor noted his history of drug abuse and his present symptoms and suggested that he be tested for HIV, along with other possibilities. Anthony reluctantly agreed. His tests showed that he was indeed HIV positive, probably infected from sharing needles in his days of doing cocaine.

Anthony becomes despondent, not only about his own diagnosis, but also with the realization that he may have infected Luisa and their unborn child. He feels ashamed, guilty, angry, and cheated. He can't believe that this is happening to him now that he has finally turned his life around. And he can't believe that this may be happening to Luisa and their child who never made the mistakes in life that he had.

Sam is on a pastoral care team with Anthony that ministers to ex-offenders. One night as he is cleaning up after a meeting, he sees Anthony slumped over, head in hands. Sam gently approaches him and asks him if he is okay. Anthony blurts out his story and tells Sam he is desperate.

> **Anthony 1:** I just don't know what to do. I know I should tell Luisa, but this will *kill* her, and our baby ... It's bad enough I did this to myself, but what if I infected them too? I'll never forgive myself.

Sam 1: I can only imagine how difficult this is for you, Anthony. Let's try to talk this out a bit and see what your options are.

Anthony 2: I don't see how that will help. I don't see that I have many options. Sometimes I think the best option is just to end things now.

Sam 2: Anthony, I have to ask you what you mean by that.

Anthony 3: You know ...

Sam 3: Tell me.

Anthony 4: Sometimes I think it would be easier for me just to die right now. But then I worry about Luisa and the baby.

Sam 4: Anthony, are you thinking of taking your own life?

Anthony 5: Yes and no.

Sam 5: Tell me about the yes part.

Anthony 6: I'm hurting so much, that seems like a good way to stop hurting.

Sam 6: Do you have any specific plan in mind?

Anthony 7: Not really. I just sometimes find myself considering that as an option.

Sam 7: Anthony, it sounds as if suicide has been one of the ideas you have had, but that you haven't put much thought into it. Tell me more about the part of you who says no to this idea.

Anthony 8: Well, I haven't given up all hope yet, and I just couldn't leave Luisa alone to face all of this.

Sam 8: So your love for Luisa and your concern for her helps to prevent you from seriously considering suicide. Anything else?

Anthony 9: Well, I know that murder is really bad and I wouldn't want to do something that was so bad. It's bad enough that I screwed up my life with drugs. I wouldn't want to end my life screwing up.

Sam 9: That sounds like another reason not to seriously consider suicide.

Anthony 10: Yeah. I guess I'm not really serious about doing it. Just sometimes it seems tempting.

Sam 10: We'll come back to that again. But let's back up a bit and see what we are dealing with. Maybe it will help to break this up into smaller parts. I imagine it seems quite overwhelming to you.

Anthony 11: It seems like my worst nightmare and I'm just waiting to wake up.

Sam 11: Wow! That's scary. Let's start with what has happened so far. When did you find out you were HIV positive?

Anthony 12: Just a few days ago. The doctor called me into his office and told me the results of the blood tests. He told me a lot of other stuff but I don't remember much of it now. I didn't really hear anything after, "I'm sorry to inform you that you are HIV positive ..."

Sam 12: I can see how that would be shocking—almost too much to bear, and how you wouldn't be able to hear beyond that.

Anthony 13: That's right.

Sam 13: But it might be helpful to try and look beyond that.

Anthony 14: What do you mean? Beyond that is death!

Sam 14: Anthony, HIV is not the quick 'death sentence it once was. There are a number of effective treatments and people are living with the disease a lot longer now.

Anthony 15: I guess I haven't even thought about treatment. I just assumed my life was over. Maybe I should know more. Is there a cure?

Sam 15: There is no cure yet, but there are good treatments that can keep symptoms manageable and your health more stable longer. Sounds like another visit to the doctor or to the AIDS clinic to talk with a counselor would be very helpful.

Anthony 16: You make it sound as if there is some hope.

Sam 16: There's always hope, Anthony. I think it is important for you to get in touch with that hope so you can continue *living* with this disease.

Anthony 17: You keep saying live, I like that. I guess I've only thought about dying.

Sam 17: It's important not to write yourself off too soon, Anthony. I know you are a survivor and a fighter—you have licked drugs and that strength and courage will help you now.

Anthony 18: But what about Luisa and the baby? It's so unfair. They didn't do anything to deserve this.

Sam 18: *No one* deserves this, Anthony. HIV infection is not a punishment; it's a disease that needs to be treated and lived with.

Anthony 19: But how do I tell Luisa about this?

Sam 19: Let's look at that step by step.

Sam is calling upon all his training in crisis and grief counseling to respond to Anthony. As Anthony begins to speak, he begins to *as-*

sess what is going on. Hearing words like "it would be easier for me to die now" and "that seems like a good way to stop hurting," he begins to think in terms of *crisis* and potential *suicide*. A *crisis* is "an individual's internal reaction to an external hazard" (Stone 13). For some, a seemingly small event will evoke a crisis reaction: getting a B on a paper has evoked a crisis reaction for some of my students, whereas getting a B on a paper has been an event to rejoice about for others. Therefore, the event itself is not a crisis; the crisis occurs *within* the person experiencing the event.

Some events, by their very nature, are more likely to evoke a crisis reaction in *any* person—such as the sudden death of a beloved child, getting fired from a needed job, and *being diagnosed as HIV positive.* Anthony's event falls into this last category and he is indeed reacting to the diagnosis with crisis behavior. Anthony sees no options and he is paralyzed with fear.

Sam is proceeding with the *first step* of crisis intervention: *assessment.*[13]

- Is there a threat to life—Anthony's or others? What is the risk of suicide, homicide, and harm?

- Is Anthony able to function on a day-to-day basis? (Hoff 79)

Having determined that Anthony is not actively suicidal, Sam continues with assessing his functioning, while he moves into *step two* of crisis counseling: *active intervention.* This step involves gathering facts and getting a picture of what has happened so far and how it has affected Anthony. Sam does this by affirming, asking information questions, sharing information, and using immediacy to draw out Anthony's strengths. (See the list of skills in the Appendix.)

- Sam 1 combines empathy with a probe.

- Sam 2, 3 and 5 are probes.

- Sam 7 and 8 summarize, then probe.

- Sam 9 is advanced empathy.

- Sam 10 is summary and empathy.

- Sam 4, 6, and 11 (last question) are information questions.

- Sam 13, 14, 15, 16, and 18 are information sharing.

- Sam 12 is an empathic response.

- Sam 17 is immediacy.

During this time Sam also challenges Anthony to reframe what he has seen as overwhelming and insurmountable obstacles as possibilities with a number of options.

The next step will be for Sam to come up with *a concrete and immediate short-term plan*. He works with Anthony to determine what he will do next. (He begins this in Sam 19.) At this point Sam is helping Anthony get through the next few hours or days so that he leaves with a clear sense of what he can do.

Finally, Sam assures Anthony that he will call the next day to see how he is, and then in a few days to see how things are going. He will make sure that he has other resource people as well. He will see if he wants to meet with him again to look at some of the bigger issues and some longer-term planning about his future, or if he prefers doing this with his doctor or an AIDS counselor. This is all part of *step four* of crisis counseling: *follow-up*.

Concurrent with experiencing a crisis, Anthony is also experiencing the first reactions of grief—shock and disbelief. Sam is aware that Anthony is experiencing loss and the threat of loss and he will need to grieve his many losses. He is also aware that HIV infection and AIDS is a complicated grief situation and Anthony will need to identify and strengthen his positive resources to help him through the complications of his illness.

Anthony does tell Luisa about being HIV positive and she is tested. She finds out that she is also HIV positive and that there is a 24 percent chance that their child will be HIV positive (Harmon 22).[14] They try to prepare for what this will mean in their lives. They both have a lot of anger—Luisa toward Anthony, and Anthony toward God—and fear. They both look to Sam for continued support and for help with their faith issues. They both receive support and counseling from the local AIDS clinic.

Sam finds that it is most important that he assure Anthony and Luisa that he will *not abandon* them in their illness, in their anger, and in their hopelessness. To do this he will have had to:

- become familiar with the disease and the challenges and complications surrounding the disease
- address his own feelings as they come up in his ministry
- identify and strengthen his own resources and supports
- come face-to-face with his own mortality
- be willing to stay with pain that he cannot fix
- nurture his own spiritual life
- watch for signs of depression and hopelessness in himself
- know that he cannot and should not be the sole support for this family

At first Anthony and Luisa do not want to share with the community about their disease. Sam honors this decision but makes sure that they have other sources of support as well. He also begins an AIDS educational program in his congregation to prepare them for present and future congregational ministry. He holds workshops on Scripture and AIDS, Basic Information about AIDS, and Counseling with People Who Are HIV Positive. He works with the staff to incorporate AIDS awareness and AIDS support into the worshiping life and mission outreach of the church. The church members look at a number of ways they can become more involved with AIDS ministry and decide to incorporate prayers for those suffering with AIDS into their weekly community prayers, set aside one Sunday a year as AIDS Ministry Sunday, support local AIDS programs, and co-sponsor a display of the AIDS quilt.

As Luisa and Anthony see their church become more understanding of their disease, they decide to share their story with them. They know that they are still taking a risk, but they also know that this is what they want to do. Some in the church are fearful and judgmental, but they are few. Many write letters or call, and as Anthony and Luisa struggle with the disease, many visit and arrange meals and help care for Maria, their daughter, who is HIV negative. As Luisa and Anthony continue to struggle with their disease, they witness a transformation taking place in their faith community. They are comforted to know that when they die, their church community will continue to minister to others with AIDS and will continue to advocate on behalf of all those affected by AIDS. Although they still pray for a cure for themselves and still sorrow in knowing Maria will be orphaned, they try to take each day as it comes and to live in the present. They find they grow closer together as a family and are able to reach out to other hurting people in ways they never thought possible.

Both Luisa and Anthony, and their community of faith, weather the complications of AIDS through awareness, support, education, prayer, and an honest working through of *all* their emotions and questions.

Abortion

Kenneth Doka places abortion under the second type of disenfranchised grief—the loss is not recognized. He argues that the abortion may take place without anyone knowing it, or without anyone approving of it, or without anyone acknowledging that an actual loss has occurred ("Hidden Sorrow" 273). Even those who believe that a loss *has* occurred may not *condone* the act, and those who accept the act may downplay the loss.

I would argue that not only does abortion fit under Doka's second type of disenfranchised grief, but it may also (concurrently) fit under types 1 (the relationship is not recognized) and 3 (the griever is not recognized). When this is true, the griever experiences a "triple whammy" (my term) of complications.

The relationship is not recognized. This type of disenfranchised grief could apply to the mother, father, or any relative or friend of the unborn child. Since a child has not actually been born, there is not a live person to have a relationship with. Only the mother (the woman carrying the child) *might* be afforded some recognition of relationship, but since she often keeps her pregnancy and abortion a secret for fear of disapproval, even she will not be granted the status of a mother who has lost a child. Certainly others who would have a relationship with the unborn and future child have even less recognized relationship status here. They may not even know that they have experienced the loss of a (potential) child, grandchild, nephew, or niece. If they do know, they may be too ashamed to divulge their loss.

The griever is not recognized. In this case the griever is defined as one who is incapable of grief. Many may think that a woman who "chooses" abortion to end the life of her child is not capable of grieving the loss of that child, since she has "purposefully" participated in ending the life. Even when abortion is her choice, she still needs to grieve her loss, and she is capable of doing so.

Abortion, then, is a difficult loss to grieve. There may be an inordinate amount of *denial* present—denial that there is a loss, or that the loss is significant, or that the loss is the death of a child or future child. Grief may be *delayed* for months or years because of the secretiveness of the act of abortion. Grief may be *triggered* by an anniversary, the birth of another child, or by another loss. Thus, grief may remain *unresolved* for years. It may also be complicated because of an inability to name, recognize, and grieve *secondary losses* that are occurring—loss of youth, loss of innocence, loss of dreams, or loss of hopes.

Mary

Mary came to me for counseling because of what she called "a depression she couldn't shake." She felt listless, sad, and unable to think clearly. When I asked her if she had experienced any recent losses, she was unable to name anything that she thought was significant. I mentioned that sometimes sadness is triggered by a sight, a sound, or a date that evokes memories that we are no longer consciously aware of. I reminded her that she had begun counseling with me on October 21 and asked her if the third week of October had any significance for her. At first her face registered nothing, then a pained and alarmed look came over her. "Oh, my God," she moaned, "of course. October twenty-fifth was the due date. How could I forget?"

Over the next few sessions Mary was able to share with me that she had become pregnant when she was very young—only thirteen. Her parents had decided that it was in her best interest to terminate the pregnancy immediately, before it was really a baby. She had her abortion in April 1980 and it was never spoken of again.

Mary was usually able to push away any feelings of sadness that came up in April each year, but she had never equated the month of October with her pregnancy. Trying to avoid any talk about her pregnancy or the child, Mary's parents had never discussed a due date or looked at the possibility of adoption. Mary was never allowed to imagine carrying the child to term or to think about a birth date. Her parents thought it best not to deal with the pregnancy at all by ending it as soon as possible. Because of her age and the circumstances of her pregnancy (she was raped by an older cousin), Mary did whatever her parents thought was best.

Now, eighteen years later, her best friend had just given birth to her first child—on October 25. Mary's delayed grief over the loss of her own child eighteen years earlier surprised and overwhelmed her.

How Do We as Pastoral Ministers Respond to Mary?

- Listen compassionately.
- Know that we may be the first and only person to ever hear this story.
- Name the abortion as loss, even death. Name the circumstances surrounding the abortion.
- Help Mary to name the many secondary losses she has experienced in relation to the abortion—loss of youth, loss of innocence, and loss of dreams.
- Encourage Mary to grieve her many losses.
- Work with Mary to develop appropriate rituals to enhance her grieving process, such as:
  - naming the child
  - writing a letter to the child
  - seeking forgiveness
  - forgiving others who contributed to the abortion—parents, doctor, cousin
  - planning a memorial service
  - contributing time or money to a children's charity in the child's name

Mary has been emotionally numb and in denial for many years. In recognizing her losses and grief, she may experience a barrage of intense feelings, particularly guilt, anger, and remorse. She will need a lot of support, understanding, forgiveness, and encouragement.

Study Questions

1. What is a disenfranchised loss? What are the three types of disenfranchised grief? Why is disenfranchised grief complicated grief?

2. Why is suicide a particularly difficult death?

3. Why are survivors of suicide reluctant to reveal that their loved one committed suicide?

4. What are the stages of suicidal grief? What additional tasks and difficulties exist at each stage?

5. What types of unresolved grief might a survivor of suicide experience?

6. Name some things that survivors of suicide can do to help themselves.

7. Name some things pastoral ministers can do to help survivors of suicide.

8. What does Scripture say about suicide?

9. What rituals might be done for survivors of suicide?

10. What can church communities do to help survivors of suicide and those contemplating suicide?

11. What are some of the unique issues that persons with AIDS and their families face?

12. What is a crisis? What are the four steps of crisis intervention?

13. What do pastoral ministers need to do to effectively minister to PWA and their families? What can church communities do?

14. Why is abortion a particularly difficult disenfranchised grief? What are some of the secondary losses involved in abortion?

Practicums

1. Have the large group strategize ways that church communities can be proactive in their ministries to survivors of suicide and persons with AIDS. Name potential issues and obstacles that arise in the planning.

2. Review the case of Anthony and Luisa. What might you have done differently? Look at the responses and skills used. Are you able to accurately identify skills? What more might Sam have said or done? Set up a role-play in which you continue the conversation.

3. Discuss how your religious views (understanding of Scripture and church doctrine) influence how you minister to a survivor of suicide, a person with AIDS, or a woman who has had an abortion.

Chapter Three

Sudden, Unanticipated Losses

This chapter focuses on complicated grief due to three types of losses: accident, homicide, and rape. All three losses have in common the sudden, unexpected, and unanticipated nature of the loss. Each loss has additional factors that contribute to complicated grieving.

According to Therese Rando, the two risk factors that contribute the *most* to complicated mourning are (*Complicated Mourning* 554):

1. the *suddenness* of the death, and

2. a relationship with the deceased that was extremely angry, ambivalent, or dependent.

This chapter focuses on the factor of *suddenness*—*why* this makes a death or loss so complicated, and *what* grievers and grief ministers can *do* to better understand and cope with this kind of loss.

A sudden death is usually *unexpected*. This catches survivors off-guard, unprepared, and defenseless. We are overwhelmed by the loss, unable to believe it has actually happened. Our coping abilities are "assaulted," and we fear for our own life as well as the lives of other loved ones, as we try to grasp and understand that our loved one is gone. We live in fearful anticipation, waiting for the proverbial other shoe to drop, for another tragic and sudden loss to occur. We are besieged by the "what ifs" of the actual loss: What if we hadn't let him drive to school? What if we had driven instead? What if he had left five minutes later? What if we had checked on her before we left for work? We are also haunted by the "what ifs" of the potential losses: What if we also die suddenly? Who will take care of the children? What if someone else we love dies, how will we go on?

Our world is shattered by the suddenness of the loss and by other factors that often accompany a sudden death:

- the death was also violent (homicide)
- the death is perceived as preventable
- the death was one of many (community disaster or multiple deaths)
- the death was random (accident)
- the death was untimely (such as a child)

Rando identifies eleven issues associated with sudden, unexpected deaths that particularly complicate the grieving process for survivors (555–556):

1. Our ability to cope is lessened. What worked in dealing with other losses and other crises does not work here.

2. Our assumptive world is rattled. The assumptive world is what we believe about the world: children bury their parents; parents are responsible for their children's lives; God protects the innocent.

3. The death seems senseless. We can find no reason for the loss: "She wasn't suffering." "He was in the prime of his life." "She was such a good person."

4. There is no chance to say good-bye. Survivors feel a lack of closure and regret at not being able to say good-bye. We feel that there is unfinished business left with the deceased.

5. The symptoms of grief persist. Because of the many complicating factors, it is difficult to "resolve" the loss and grief may become *chronic*.

6. There is a tendency on the part of survivors to continually, even obsessively, reconstruct the events surrounding the death. We try to regain control by understanding how the death happened. This may be helpful, but it may also be harmful—particularly if we blame ourselves for what we did or did not do in the chain of events leading to the death.

7. Survivors feel a loss of security about the world. We fear other losses and are afraid to reinvest in other relationships and in life in general.

8. The sudden, unexpected loss cuts across everything in our lives and relationship with the deceased, highlighting only what happened and what the relationship was like at the time of death. This "time freeze" often focuses only on the negative—what we did *not* say or do. This is a distortion of perception.

9. Our feelings are more intense and more difficult to deal with for us and for pastoral ministers who work with us.

10. Sudden death is followed by a number of secondary losses, such as loss of income, loss of role, and loss of a future or past generation.

11. Sudden, unexpected death can provoke a *post-traumatic stress response*, which may intensify grieving. This will need to be addressed *before* the grieving can be addressed. (See page 66 for more information on post-traumatic stress response.)

A sudden death may also occur within a terminal illness when death *is* expected, but at a later date. Some of the complicating factors of sudden death will not be present, but any and all could be present. Also, an anticipated death may be just as *painful* for survivors as a sudden death. The biggest difference between a sudden, unexpected death and a protracted, anticipated death will be in the *diminishment of the ability to cope* by the survivors of sudden death (Rando, *How to Go on Living* 89–90). The survivors are overwhelmed.

An abundance of literature points to the benefit of having advance warning of a death (Fulton and Fulton; Glick et al.; Parkes; Parkes and Weiss). Advanced warning allows grievers time to address unfinished business, to prepare for the death, and to absorb the reality of the loss (Rando, *Grief, Dying and Death* 51–52). A study done on widows by Glick, Weiss, and Parkes in 1974 found that when widows did not have sufficient time to do *anticipatory grieving*—because of the suddenness of the death of their husband—they did not remarry. Those widows with adequate warning were more likely to remarry. However, there was no difference in the *depth* of the grief.

Sudden, unanticipated loss interferes particularly with the first "R" process, recognizing the loss, and with the fifth and sixth "R" processes, readjusting and reinvesting. Sudden loss may also result in *unanticipated grief*, when survivors experience extreme feelings, are unable to function, and when these grief symptoms persist over time.

Sudden Death: Accident

George

George (38) had been married to Susan (37) for fifteen years. They met in college and married right after graduation. They had delayed having children while they built their careers, bought their first house, and traveled extensively. In their mid-thirties, feeling financially secure, and with a solid and loving relationship, they decided to have a child. Although it took Susan almost three years to conceive, they were now expecting their first child at Christmas.

Susan had been tiring easily and decided to take a day off from work to shop, and then to relax and sleep. She asked George if he could join her and make a "fun" day of it. "It may be the last time we shop alone together for a long time," Susan reminded him. George did not see the humor in this. Lately he was feeling insecure about having a child after so many years of childless, married life. He was also feeling overwhelmed at work. "How can you *joke* about it," he asked Susan. "You know how stressed I am at work, and about the baby. And I *hate* shopping. You go, but don't expect me to come, too." He was sorry after he said it, but didn't say so. They went to sleep without speaking.

The next morning George was up early for a meeting. He wondered if he should wake Susan up to apologize, but then thought it was better to let her sleep; they could talk that night. He could come home early and surprise her—maybe even meet her at the mall. She would like that. He went off to work feeling much better.

He tried calling Susan that morning but no one answered. He assumed she must have left to go shopping. At 3:00 he tried again and there was still no answer. He decided to head home and surprise Susan by getting home before her. On his way home he listened to the radio. They reported an accident on the interstate that was tying up traffic, so he went home by an alternate route. He reached home by 3:30 and Susan was not there. By 4:00 he became irritated. "How much shopping can one person do?" he wondered. He began to feel justified in refusing to go with her and angry with her for being gone so long. "Probably spending too much money," he thought. At 4:30 the phone rang. He was fuming. "Hello!" he snapped, "where are you?" (He was sure it was Susan.) The voice at the other end of the line was an unfamiliar one—formal, and rather stiff. "Mr. Franklin?" (*A solicitor*, he thought.) "Yes, who is this?" "Mr. Franklin, I am very sorry to tell you this (George felt his chest constrict) but your wife has been in an accident. Could you come to County Hospital right away?"

By the time George arrived at the hospital, Susan and the baby had already died.

It is now six months later. George remains overwhelmed by the death of his wife and child. He blames himself for not going with her, for not being with her that day. He goes through the details of their last night together over and over: "If only I had said I was sorry; if only I had gone with her; if only I had said, Stay home and rest and we'll shop on the weekend ..."

George finds himself depressed—unable to cope with even the daily activities of life. He is struggling at work, but refuses to take a leave because work is the only reason for getting up in the morning. At the insistence of his mother, he attends a meeting of a bereavement group at his church. You are the pastoral minister who is the facilitator of the group.[1]

How Do You Respond to George? What Will Help You As You Minister to George?

Pastoral ministers, relatives, grief counselors, and chaplains may *all* feel *overwhelmed* when hearing of a sudden, unanticipated loss with multiple complicating factors, such as what George experienced. For most of us—grievers *or* ministers—such a loss is *not* an everyday experience, and it helps that we are *not* besieged with such difficult losses on a daily basis. But for some grief ministers, in particular hospital chaplains, sudden, unanticipated loss *will* be a common experience.

Rando and others have written about the diminishment in survivors' (and I would add *ministers'*) coping abilities, making the grieving (and I would add *ministering*) all the more difficult. The sudden, unexpected death is also an assault to our theological beliefs, and our faith—what Rando might call our "assumptive world." With each sudden and unexpected death, ministers may become *less* certain about God's power and providence (Dykstra 151). We too will be faced with such questions as: *Who* is God? *Why* does God allow this? Robert Dykstra, a hospital chaplain, suggests that it will be in the very "strangeness" of the situation that chaplains find sanctuary. I would add that it is in the extraordinariness of the event that ministers *and* grievers will find strength, comfort, and hope. Our Judeo-Christian tradition points to "strange" (extraordinary) occurrences and "strange" (extraordinary) symbols that become bearers of God's presence and promise (150): the burning bush that is not consumed, the blinding vision, the visitors at Sarah's tent, the woman at the well, the prostitutes and tax collectors, and the cross.

To effectively minister to George, pastoral ministers will need to:

- examine our own faith beliefs and confront the reality of our own and others' deaths

- learn how to not be overwhelmed by the suddenness of another's loss

- find a way to detach without being detached

- be aware of the factors that surround and complicate sudden loss

- be patient with the survivor's need to repeat details surrounding the loss, while recognizing when this repetition is part of chronic grief

- be prepared to deal with the intensity of feelings in sudden loss

- be willing to stay with the intense pain without trying to take the pain away and make the survivor "feel better"

- be willing to work with the survivor on issues surrounding the death, such as an overly dependent relationship with the deceased

- know when to refer to professional help when the grief is very complicated or when the grief is intertwined with post-traumatic stress responses

- be willing to be a resource for the theological and faith questions that will emerge from the loss

- not try to find meaning in the loss before the survivor is ready to do so

- have the necessary resources to replenish, renew, and refresh ourselves (good diet, sufficient exercise, friendships, supervision and support systems, a healthy spiritual life, and time for replenishment, vacations and retreats)

The following is a conversation that George had with his pastoral minister trained in grief counseling on the anniversary of Susan's death:

Valerie 1: Today is the one-year anniversary of Susan's death. How are you doing?

George 1: I feel like it was yesterday. The last year has been horrible. It's been like living in a fog. You know what I mean.

Valerie 2: Tell me more what *you* mean by it. What's it like for *you*?

George 2: Well, one day is just like another—nothing to look forward to, no one to come home to. I can't remember simple things—like phone numbers—but I remember every single word I said to Susan the night before she died.

Valerie 3: We've talked about that before. You carry a lot of guilt with you about the accident. You seem to feel partly responsible for Susan's death.

George 3: I am! If it wasn't for me ...

Valerie 4: If it wasn't for you, what?

George 4: It's too horrible to say!

Valerie 5: Perhaps saying it will *help.*

George 5: You'll think I'm terrible.

Valerie 5: I assure you George, nothing you say will make me think that.

George 6: Oh, I can't stand keeping it in any longer. I've thought it for so long. If it weren't for me, Susan would still be alive.

Valerie 6: I don't understand, George. How is that so?

George 7: If I had gone shopping with her, this would never have happened. There would have been no accident. It's all my fault.

Valerie 7: George, I can hear you are in great pain and distress over this. Would you be willing to talk more about it?

George 8: I'm afraid to, but I'm also afraid not to. I am so tired of keeping this all in. No one knows of the fight I had with Susan the night before she died. Everyone thinks we were the perfect couple, that I was so good to her. They don't know how I refused to go shopping with her, or how I wouldn't even talk to her the morning she died. If they knew that they'd hate me and they'd blame me, too. I can't stand how nice her parents are to me. If they only knew …

Valerie 8: It sounds as if you think you deserve to be punished for Susan's death and that you don't deserve the care that you have received.

George 9: You've got that right.

Valerie 9: Let's talk some more about this because it's important and it is certainly causing you a great deal of distress.

George 10 (reluctantly): Okay.

Valerie 10: Let me ask you where you think God fits into all of this?

George 11: What do you mean?

Valerie 11: Well, if you think you are solely responsible for Susan's death, I'm wondering what you think God's role was in her death.

George 12: Well, *he*[2] didn't argue with Susan.

Valerie 12: No, God didn't, but then where was God when you and Susan argued and when Susan had her accident?

George 13: Well, he certainly didn't do anything to help, did he?

Valerie 13: So, you're saying God had a part in this too, by *not* helping.

George 14: I don't like the sound of that, but yeah, I guess that's what I'm saying. I mean, maybe it was my fault, but God could have helped!

Valerie uses a combination of skills in listening to George:

- Valerie 1 is an open probe, asking to see where George is.

- Valerie 2 is also a probe, encouraging George to expand on his feelings from his perspective.

- Valerie 3 could be called advanced empathy. Valerie uses the word "guilt" and "responsibility" to name what George is implying. She is not afraid to name the difficult feelings that George is expressing.

- Valerie 4 is a statement of encouragement; it might be considered a prompt.

- Valerie 5 may be considered information sharing.

- Valerie 6 reflects her willingness to stay with difficult material. She encourages George to explain what he means (probe).

- Valerie 7 expresses empathy to let George know that she hears his pain. Then Valerie asks permission to go on (information question).

- Valerie 8 is advanced empathy, once again naming what George is hinting at.

- Valerie 9 encourages George to continue, while also providing information ("this is important").

- Valerie 10 is a probe, with a specific agenda—bringing in issues of God, faith, and theology. Whereas in secular counseling, the counselor will wait for the client to bring up anything theological, in pastoral care and counseling,[3] the pastoral minister has the prerogative to *initiate* a theological conversation.

- Valerie 11 summarizes what George said, and then probes.

- Valerie 12 asks an information question.

- Valerie 13 summarizes through empathy (may also be considered advanced empathy—stating what is implicit).

These responses are one set of *possible* responses. There is no *one* right response to any statement. Other counselors may have used different skills and different responses. What is important here is that:

- Valerie is not afraid to get into intense feelings and thorny theological questions.

- She gently and carefully encourages George to articulate his worst fears and to name his self-blame.

- She *begins* the process of helping George look at what he believes, who he holds responsible, and whether his beliefs are rational or irrational.

- She is not afraid of staying with George's troublesome feelings.

- She resists the temptation to try to make things all better for George; this is not helpful and it is not within her power.

- She uses her knowledge of the complications present in sudden deaths to provide information and to be aware of the potential problems.

In verbalizing his feelings, thoughts, and beliefs, George is able to see that he alone is *not* totally responsible for Susan's death. At first he feels relieved just to know that he is not solely responsible. Eventually he is able to see that a number of factors contributed to Susan's accident. He is able to express anger at the circumstances, at God, and even at Susan. He comes to believe that his actions did not cause Susan's death, and he does not need to be punished for it.

Valerie is able to talk with George about the concept of "time freeze"—in a sudden, unanticipated death survivors tend to focus *only* on the moments right before death. Valerie is able to encourage George to look at his *whole* relationship with Susan—the many happy times together, the love they shared, and how past arguments were resolved. George is able to remember that he had a quick temper that Susan was well aware of, and that Susan never carried a grudge about it. She had learned to let George flare up and cool down, and realize he had overreacted. George remembers Susan would often laugh at his outbursts, telling him, "Don't worry, that didn't bother me. I know you occasionally need to yell."

In remembering this, George is able to *reframe* the events leading up to Susan's death. Although he still needs to forgive himself for not apologizing to her or for not taking the day off, he is able to see that Susan probably did not spend the day feeling angry with him. She loved shopping and probably had a great time that day. Rather than living with unpardonable guilt and responsibility for causing his wife's death, George now carries appropriate remorse for not apologizing for his outburst. With Valerie's help, he writes a letter of apology to Susan and brings it to her grave and reads it to her. He also seeks forgiveness for his anger. After continued conversation and prayer, and with the guidance of his minister, George concludes that to "atone" for his anger he will always try to apologize before the sun sets on any argument.

Sudden Death: Homicide

Another type of sudden, unanticipated death with its own complicating factors (in addition to those already mentioned) is *homicide*.[4] Rando lists six factors that complicate grieving after a homicide (Rando, *Complicated Mourning* 540). Some factors are the same as those that exist if death is the result of a traffic accident (Susan's death). I put an asterisk (*) next to those I see as additional complicating factors:

1. suddenness, lack of anticipation

2. violence, trauma, and horror *

3. preventability

4. anger, guilt, self-blame, and shattered assumptions

5. randomness

6. secondary victimization—a revictimization of the victim or the survivor by those he or she thought would be helpful or supportive *

Further complications in a homicide might include that the person committing the homicide is someone known to the victim, and therefore also to the survivors. Three out of five murders are committed by a friend, relative, lover, colleague, or neighbor (Kastenbaum, *Society* 209).

Michalowski (87–91) describes five dimensions that make a homicide even more complicated than a death due to a traffic accident:

Dimension	Homicide	Traffic accident
1. Inevitability	Usually not seen as an accident	Usually viewed as an accident
2. Controllability	Seen as within control of the murderer—a willful act	Seen as not within person's control
3. Intent	By definition, involves intent	Seldom premeditated (may be different now with road rage)

4. Deviance	Illegal, abnormal	Normal, context of everyday living
5. Social utility	Not acceptable or helpful to society; guns and knives not necessary to society	Cars—necessary to society; consequences tolerated

Violent or mutilating deaths (homicides) are more difficult because our previous aggressive fantasies about the deceased (which we all experience) may evoke guilt after death. Violent death makes us confront the aggressiveness of humanity, and the destructiveness of humankind. According to Therese Rando in *Treatment of Complicated Mourning*, this confrontation violates our assumptive world in which humanity is not aggressive or destructive (569).

Homicides may also be characterized as *traumas* or *traumatic losses*. Traumas or traumatic losses are characterized in two ways (577):

1. as a major disaster—a bombing, internment in a concentration camp, a war, floods, or an airplane crash—horrific events that happen to and affect a large number of people; and

2. as a personal disaster experience—an event experienced by and affecting one individual as trauma.

Any death may be *subjectively* defined as traumatic (570). However, there are certain circumstances that are considered *objectively* traumatic because they are associated with factors that enhance complicated grief (509–510):

- a death that is sudden and unanticipated
- a death that involves violence, mutilation, and destruction
- a death that is viewed as preventable or random
- a death that is part of multiple deaths
- a death where survivors personally experience a threat to life or experience a confrontation with death of others

Deaths associated with these five factors can objectively be called traumatic deaths and will tend to evoke post-traumatic responses (PTSD)[5] in the survivor.

There are some key similarities between the trauma experience in a personal disaster and a more widespread (major) disaster (Raphael 331, 350):

• shock and denial

• distress

• helplessness

• death and destruction (including fear of personal death)

• images of the trauma

Judith Herman describes psychological trauma as an event that is perceived as an acute, overwhelming threat; the core experience is one of disempowerment and disconnection; core feelings include helplessness and intense fear. There is a loss of control, feeling of isolation, threat of annihilation, threats to life or bodily integrity, and a close, personal experience with violence or death (33).

Persons with PTSD probably need intervention and help beyond what most pastoral ministers can provide. However, pastoral ministers need to be able to *identify* PTSD, understand which events are likely to be objectively traumatic, and remain in supportive pastoral relationships with survivors.

Ministry with persons with PTSD will proceed through a number of processes. According to Rando (*Complicated Mourning* 589–590), caregivers (ministers) will need to:

• establish a trusting relationship

• provide information about PTSD and grief

• focus on the symptoms of PTSD and the defenses and behaviors used against (distancing and distortion) or to control (acting out and self-medication) symptoms

• focus on skills for alternative responses: assertiveness and problem-solving

• help to recollect and integrate trauma memories into a new identity and life

• help in managing stress and mourning

Judith Herman describes the process of recovery from trauma as occurring in three stages: safety, remembrance and mourning, and reconnection (155). Pastoral ministers alone may not be qualified to counsel persons with PTSD through all these stages, but we can collaborate with professional therapists[6] to assist with shepherding and supporting our parishioner in recovery. We will be especially helpful with the theological aspects of recovery. For many, the experience of a personal or more widespread trauma will evoke a crisis of faith, shattering the connection we have with God and/or with a community. Our sense of basic trust is shattered and we must relearn to trust in ourselves, others, and God (55–59). In addition to working with professional counselors, pastoral ministers will need to call on communities of faith. According to Herman, a person's community is pivotal in acknowledging that a trauma has occurred, in naming who is responsible for the harm, and in atoning for injury. Recognition and restitution are essential in restoring the survivors' need for order and justice, and allowing us to move on in our recovery (70).

One type of ritual that has evolved surrounding deaths that are violent and unanticipated is *spontaneous memorialization*—a public, community response to death (such as placing flowers or special items at a site). This memorialization usually takes place at the site of death, or at a site significant to the deceased (Kastenbaum, *Society* 376).

Rape

Andrea: A Case of Date Rape

At nineteen, Andrea felt "on top of the world." She had just started classes at the college of her choice, had made the varsity soccer team as a freshman, and was dating Kevin, the cutest guy on campus (everyone said so). For years she had felt shy and insecure—never pretty enough, never athletic enough, never smart enough. But now that everything was going so well, she was beginning to believe maybe she was okay. On her fifth date with Kevin he asked her to date only him; he wanted them to be an "exclusive couple." She couldn't believe her good luck. Of course she agreed. One night, a few weeks later, Kevin was walking her back to her dorm after studying together at the library. About halfway to her dorm Kevin wanted to stop and talk. "I'm tired, Kev, can it wait?" She usually agreed to whatever Kevin wanted, but she was really tired. "No, we need to talk now!" he demanded.

Months later, when telling about that night, she keys into this moment. She says in her heart she knew that she had a *right* to say how she felt and that in the last few weeks she had continually backed away from doing this because of the reaction she would see in Kevin when she tried to assert herself. In trying to remember what happens next, she thinks she must have been startled by Kevin's anger and backed away from him. Kevin seemed to soften and put his arms around her, kissing her. "Maybe we don't need to talk," he whispered, "we just need to be close." Inside herself Andrea once again felt a need to assert herself, but she was afraid Kevin would become angry again. Besides, she liked being held and kissed. As Kevin's kisses became more insistent and passionate, Andrea began to feel uncomfortable. She tried backing away from him, but he only drew her closer. She tried to tell him to stop, but he wasn't listening. She felt herself freezing up. Somehow they were now on the ground and Kevin was pulling off her pants. She looked around, hoping someone would be nearby, but she knew it was late and they were in an isolated part of the campus. She tried reasoning with Kevin, but he insisted this was right—that it was good for her—and that she wanted it too. She stopped speaking and felt herself drift away. What did it matter? She felt numb. She felt nothing. When it was over, Kevin said to her, "See I told you it would be good!" What could she say?

She returned to the dorm and went right to bed. Two days later her roommate found her on the floor of the bathroom, unconscious, with a bottle of pills by her side.

In her follow-up counseling for attempted suicide, Andrea never told her counselor about the rape. She talked about the pressure of school, getting good grades, and doing well in soccer. She claimed she didn't know *what* came over her that night—it had never happened before and it would certainly never happen again. Everyone wondered why she broke up with Kevin. But most of the girls were happy that he was once again available. After her first semester Andrea transferred to a smaller college five hundred miles away. She stopped playing soccer and kept to herself. She made it through her first year and went home for the summer.

Her parents are concerned about her transfer, her social withdrawal, and her quitting soccer, but can't figure out what is wrong. They ask Patty, their youth minister, to talk with Andrea.

Andrea sees Patty for a few sessions and Andrea talks about school—her classes, what she is majoring in, and what she hopes to do after finishing her degree. She avoids all talk about the transfer, quitting soccer, or keeping to herself.

One day, Andrea calls Patty and says she must see her right away. Patty agrees to see her within the hour.

When Andrea walks into Patty's office, she is highly agitated and anxious. She has a newspaper clipping with her and she asks Patty to read it. Patty reads a story about the arrest of a college student who is charged with rape. Patty realizes that the college is the one that Andrea transferred from.

Andrea is able to tell Patty about her rape. The story comes out in bits and pieces with little affect. Patty knows that she is not a professional counselor, and she realizes that Andrea needs the expertise of a professional counselor. Patty is able to continue to work with Andrea in a supportive, pastoral relationship, in collaboration with her professional counselor.

Patty is helped in her work with Andrea by understanding that rape is a complicated, traumatic loss. She realizes that Andrea's grief may take many forms, particularly the form of unresolved grief that Rando calls *unanticipated grief*—grief that occurs after a sudden, unanticipated loss. Grievers experience a sense of disruptiveness, but cannot fully comprehend the loss. We are bewildered and anxious, suffer from self-reproach and depression, and cannot function. The grief stays with us for a long time. Andrea's grief is further complicated because her loss is also *ambiguous* and *disenfranchised*. It is *ambiguous* because Andrea is having trouble recognizing that a loss has occurred (the first "R" process) and because her loss is not recognized by society. This is partly because Andrea has been unwilling to share her loss; some of this ambiguity might be cleared up when she shares her story and her losses are recognized. It is *disenfranchised* because her loss is not recognized and she herself is not recognized as a griever. Andrea feels caught here. Some of the complications can be addressed in the telling of her story so that she and her losses can be recognized, and her losses can be named. Yet because rape evokes both compassion *and* judgment, sympathy *and* misunderstanding, her losses may continue to be ambiguous and disenfranchised.

Patty realizes that Andrea is also likely to experience PTSD. Because of this Patty will need to attend to Andrea's need to:

- feel safe
- reestablish trust in the world
- rebuild an assumptive world that has been shattered
- deal with the why questions (Why me? Why did God allow this to happen?)
- act out her fantasy of revenge
- reconstruct events surrounding the rape
- focus on the moment of the rape itself
- transform her traumatic memories

Patty does this in collaboration with Andrea's counselor and as a representative of a community of faith that requires each one of us to "do justice, and to love kindness, and to walk humbly with your God" (Mi 6:8b [NRSV]).

Study Questions

1. Why is a sudden death particularly difficult? What factors that accompany sudden death contribute to complications?

2. What "R" processes do unanticipated losses interfere with? What type of unresolved grief can sudden death result in?

3. Describe how sudden death assaults our "assumptive world."

4. How can pastoral ministers more effectively minister to survivors of sudden death?

5. What is a time freeze? How does this affect the survivor's ability to grieve a sudden death?

6. Name three factors that complicate grieving after a homicide.

7. How can death by homicide be experienced as more complicated than death by traffic accident?

8. What is a trauma? What are two different types of trauma? How are they similar/different?

9. What can pastoral ministers do to better minister to persons experiencing PTSD? What can communities of faith do?

10. Why is rape a particularly difficult loss? Under what type of loss might it be classified?

11. How can pastoral ministers effectively minister to women who have been raped?

Practicums

1. Break into groups of three. One person will be the survivor of a sudden death, one person will be the pastoral minister, and one person will be the observer. Have the survivor role-play a recent, sudden loss. Counsel for ten minutes. Have the observer give feedback.

   ◆ What was difficult?

   ◆ What was helpful?

   ◆ What feelings did the survivor experience? What feelings did the minister experience?

   ◆ How did your knowledge of complicated loss help or hinder you?

   ◆ What more did you feel you needed to know to be more effective in your ministry?

2. Set up a similar role-play with a survivor of rape. Before doing the role-play, prayerfully reflect on Micah 6:8: "What does the Lord require of you but to do justice, and to love kindness, and to walk humbly with your God."

   ◆ Was the client able to talk about the experience?

   ◆ What hindered you as a minister?

   ◆ How did your consideration of Micah 6:8 affect your response as a minister?

Chapter Four

Children and Death

This chapter will focus on three experiences of children and death: (1) from the perspective of the parents who lose a child, (2) from the perspective of a child who loses a sibling, and (3) from the perspective of a child who loses a parent.

Parental Loss of a Child

The parental loss of a child is one of the most complicated grieving situations any of us will ever face. The grief from this loss is particularly intense and long lasting for a number of reasons (Rando, "Bereaved Parents" 119–131; *How to Go on Living* 161–198; and *Complicated Mourning* 611–631):

- The parent-child relationship is the most intense of our lives and the resulting grief from the loss of this relationship is equally intense.

- The death of a child is felt as a threat to our own sense of immortality as parents.

- The child's death is seen as a threat to our function and duty as parents—to protect the child and preserve the family.

- The death of a child is unnatural; it is out of sequence, untimely. We believe that we will be buried by our children, not that we will bury our children.

- The death of a child is a death of our present reality and a loss of hopes and dreams for our future.

- The death of a child causes us to experience survivor guilt, and to feel victimized. It tears into our dreams and our self-esteem.

- The death of a child affects our marital-parental relationship; we as parents grieve differently because of gender, and personality, and differ in our ability to communicate our grief.

- As parents we experience unique upsurges of grief. In addition to the grief that arises at holidays, we will experience grief at the dates when our child would have gone to school, attended the prom, or graduated.

- We experience a sense of failure—failing in our parental role to care for our child.

- We experience an assault on our identity as a parent; this is especially true in the death of an only child.

- We lose a part of ourselves and experience intense separation pain; it is like part of our very self is ripped out.

- We experience a number of secondary losses, including the loss of the family as it once was, and the loss of future caretakers.

- There is no word to describe us as grieving parents—like widow, widower, or orphan.

- Others stigmatize and avoid us because we represent their worst fears.

- The death of a child is often sudden, further complicating the grieving process.

- The child's death is often seen as preventable.

- We are left with an overwhelming sense of unfinished business.

- There may be resentment toward other living children for surviving. There may be a lessening of intensity in relationships with surviving children because we fear the pain of losing another child. We may become overprotective or ambiguous toward surviving children.

- Difficulties in the six "R" processes may occur, particularly in relinquishing attachment to the old assumptive world because we are forced to revise the most basic assumptions about being adult parents.

- Although we tend to equate the difficulty in grieving the death of a child with age, the age of the child is on the one hand irrelevant, in that whatever the age of the child—five, fifteen, or fifty—the dynamics of parental grief apply. On the other hand, age does matter in that different complicating factors are present at different ages.

Danny

At four years old, Danny was trying to do everything his older brother, Todd, was doing. Danny adored Todd and couldn't understand why eight-year-old Todd did not want to include Danny in his play. One summer day Danny and Todd were playing in the front yard while their mother, Dana, was doing dishes inside. She wanted to finish cleaning up before taking the boys to the playground. She asked Todd to be nice to Danny "just for a few minutes, and then we'll be on our way."

She could see the boys from the window and knew they wouldn't wander from the yard. She could see Danny following Todd around, imitating everything Todd did. For once, Todd seemed to be enjoying Danny's attention. She could hear them playing "follow the leader"—Danny valiantly trying to keep up with Todd. She thought to herself, "This is a good day. This is how it is supposed to be. It is so good to see them get along and to hear their laughter."

She too found herself laughing at Danny as he jumped, ran, and strutted—just like Todd.

She saw them climb up to the tree house. Todd never let Danny go up there with him. This was great! Then she heard Danny's voice, "Let me be the leader, now. Jump."

As she watched she saw Danny smiling, and laughing, and shouting as he jumped from the tree house. She felt a tug at her heart. "That's pretty high up," she thought. "I hope he doesn't break his leg." She watched Danny fall to the ground and then she heard a loud thud, and then nothing. As she ran out the door she saw Danny's small body lying very still on the ground. Todd was climbing down from the tree house. She told him to go inside and dial 911 and tell them to send an ambulance to their house.

Somehow Dana knew that something was terribly wrong. Danny was lying so still. She went over to him and called his name. No response. She was afraid to move him but she was more afraid not to. She felt for his pulse. There was none. She began CPR, yelling to Todd to run next door for help. She continued CPR until the ambulance arrived.

The doctors said it was a "freak" accident. Danny broke his neck and was killed instantly. There was nothing anyone could have done. Dana took no comfort in those words. She felt *she* could have prevented the accident. "If only we had left earlier, this wouldn't have happened. I had to do the damn dishes!"

In the months following Danny's death, you (Jude, the Director of Religious Education) have the occasion to see Ron (the father), Dana, and Todd often. They remain active in church, seeking comfort in their faith. They join a support group for bereaved parents. Dana approaches you wanting to talk. Todd's religious education teacher overheard him saying that if he hadn't been so nice to Danny that day, he wouldn't have died. He thinks that maybe we shouldn't be nice to each other, because if we are, the person might die. Dana is concerned and asks your advice on how to address this.

Dana 1: Jude, thanks for seeing me on such short notice. This has thrown me for a loop. I have done everything I could to assure Todd that Danny's death was an accident and he was not at fault. Who knew he would think he was to blame because *he was nice*!

Jude 1: Dana, it does sound a bit odd, but eight year olds reason differently than we do.

Dana 2: I know. I was warned that Todd might blame himself for bad thoughts, but not for good thoughts!

Jude 2: Dana, I know that you and Ron have joined a support group for parents who have lost a child. What about Todd?

Dana 3: Oh, he is part of a group for siblings. I know I can talk to the facilitator of that group. And I will. But there is more to this than Todd's comment. I'm actually more concerned about two other things: what the teacher said to Todd and how Ron is dealing with this.

Jude 3: Dana, please go on. I don't know about either of these things.

Dana 4: First, the teacher's comment. She said to Todd that God only chooses the best to be with God. No wonder Todd thinks he shouldn't be good.

Jude 4: I had no idea, Dana. That was certainly not a helpful comment and I will talk with Marge about it.

Dana 4: Thanks. And then there is Ron. He doesn't talk about Danny at all—not that I know of. He has taken on more responsibility at work and is keeping very long hours. We hardly see each other.

Even in this brief interaction we can see a number of issues arising:

1. When faced with a difficult death, many people try to be helpful by offering what they think are "comforting phrases." Marge's comment that "God only takes the best" is one of these types of phrases.

   Other "comforting phrases" that are used at the time of death include:

   - She's with God now.

   - His time was up.

   - It was God's will.

   - You're young, you'll have other children.

   - God never gives us more that we can bear.

   - It was part of God's plan.

   - For everything there is a season ... a time to be born and a time to die (Eccl 3:1a, 2a [NRSV]).

   - She's gone to take care of other little boys and girls in heaven.

   - God needed him more than we did.

   You may add to this list. As dreadful as many of these phrases sound, we who utter them usually mean well. Our intention is to make grievers feel better, and to provide some sort of explanation or meaning to what seems like a senseless death. I have found that *none of these phrases are helpful for pastoral ministers to use*. These phrases are only useful when coming from grievers trying to make sense of a child's death.

2. Jude noted the possibility of the gender differences that might be occurring in the different ways Dana and Ron were expressing their grief.

   Carol Staudacher breaks the grieving process into three phases or reactions (4):

   - retreating

- working through

- resolving

Men *appear* to go from phase 1 to phase 3 quicker; women *appear* to stay longer in phase 2 (8). There are many reasons for this. Women are *allowed, encouraged,* and more often *comfortable* with expressing their emotions through crying and talking. Some men are also comfortable in expressing their feelings in this way, but society does not often encourage this overt expression in men. Men are expected to "be strong," which seems to be equated with not expressing sadness. Men are treated differently after death. After Danny's death, people would come up to Ron and Dana and ask *only* Dana, "How are you doing?" There is really only one way to grieve, however, regardless of gender: *We must all go through the various emotions, reactions, tasks, and challenges of grieving.* Even if men *seem* to do this "quicker" or differently, they are still left with all the feelings of grief that need to be worked through. Where does a man's grief go? How does it find expression? Staudacher suggests five coping styles that men use (9):

- remaining silent

- mourning in secret

- doing physical activity, or taking legal action

- becoming immersed in activity

- exhibiting addictive behavior

Being aware of these potential differences can alert couples and counselors to potential problem areas in the way a couple grieves.

3. Todd is still struggling with *survivor guilt* and *magical thinking.* As an eight year old, he is at the age where he personifies death as a ghost or boogieman—someone who snatches children away. He struggles with being alive, while his brother is dead (survivor guilt). He is also showing signs of magical thinking, believing that "because I was so nice, God took Danny." This may also take the form of "because I wished Danny dead, he is," and "if I wish hard enough, Danny will come back to life." This is normal, post-death thinking for an eight year old, but it needs to be watched and

responded to. Other things to watch for that may require more active and professional intervention include: excessive confusion, excessive assumption of responsibility, unexpressed feelings, isolating because of blaming self for death, extreme regression, serious difficulties at school, extreme changes in sleeping or eating, and irrational fears (Crenshaw 69–92).

4. Family members have their own unique grief and unique grieving factors: age, relationship, gender, grieving style, and personality. However, it is important not only to minister to each individual in the family, but also to realize that this is a *family* in grief who will need to grieve the loss of Danny *as a family*. This will be addressed on page 80 with the case of the Greene family.

In summary, here are important aspects for pastoral ministers to be aware of when ministering to grieving parents:

- Be aware of the tendency for others to withdraw from grieving parents.

- Be aware of the multitude of complicating factors that occur with the death of a child.

- Think about and work through the experience and meaning of the death of children *before* being faced with this situation. Consider *what* we believe and how a child's death affects this belief, our relationship with God, and our beliefs about the world.

- Remember that "silence can be golden" and is certainly to be preferred to the "comforting" phrases on page 77. Presence, caring, listening, and a willingness to stay with the pain are pivotal.

- Know that we are not alone in our ministering to the grieving parents. Call upon God, the broader community, and the community of faith for resources, support, encouragement, and love.

- Encourage and work with others to provide lifelong education and support through preaching, adult education, workshops, and support groups.

Death of a Sibling

The death of a sibling is a particularly traumatic experience for children because it enhances their awareness—probably for the first time—that they can and will die, too. The death of a sibling will also change the role and place of the surviving children in a family. The surviving siblings may become the only child, the oldest child, the youngest child, or the favorite child. If surviving siblings are younger than the child who dies, it may be especially difficult when the survivors reach the age at which the sibling died.

Although quite a bit has been written about bereaved *parents*, little research or writing has focused on bereaved *siblings*. As with the death of an adult, the death of a child will evoke various reactions depending on the type of the loss, the relationship with the deceased, gender, age, available support, and other complicating and supporting factors. Children may experience the death of a sibling through accident, illness, stillbirth, or miscarriage. Like any sudden death, an accident will have the added complicating factors of unanticipated loss (see Chapter Three). A long illness has its own complications—such as jealousy, guilt, helplessness, magical thinking, focus on the sick child to the neglect of others, overly protective parents, overly permissive parents, pressure on survivors to be perfect, pressure on survivors to take the place of the deceased, and withdrawal of friends. Miscarriages and stillbirths also have their own complications, the greatest being not treating the loss as a death and not being informed of the death.

The first part of this chapter incorporated a younger child's reaction to the death of his brother. The following case will look at the reactions of older children to the death of a sibling, as well as comment on the need to minister to the family as a whole.

The Greene Family

The Greene family consists of five living members: Tina (45), the mother; Louis (48), the father; and the children, Celeste (19), Hal (17), and Ted (13). Six months earlier Celeste's twin sister Celine took an overdose of sleeping pills and died. Celeste had been with Celine right before the suicide and had argued with her, telling her she was selfish and mean. Celeste blames herself for Celine's death, believing she pushed her over the edge. Celeste is beside herself with guilt that her father is telling her she shouldn't feel. Louis is trying to help Celeste get on with her life, and has suggested she get involved with a service group at church that he himself has joined. Hal seems to have gone on with his life, though he talks little with anyone in the family about the death. He is involved with sports and a band and is rarely home. Ted stays in his room a lot, listening to music and playing on his computer.

Celeste calls you, a minister at her church, saying she is afraid because lately she has had thoughts of taking her own life. She is also concerned about her mother, who remains secluded, and will not talk with anyone. Celeste is distraught because her mother refuses to talk with her since the death and Celeste fears that Tina blames her for Celine's death.

Individual Grief: Age and Gender-Related Responses

Each family member is responding to Celine's death from where they are as individuals. It is important to look at how various factors affect their grieving. According to Robert Kastenbaum in "Death and Development," *four* principal variables affect children's grief (25–26):

1. developmental level,

2. life experiences,

3. individual personality, and

4. patterns of communication and support.

To this list I would add gender. Three of these variables will be considered for the Greene children: gender, developmental level, and patterns of communication and support.

There are three basic questions that children (post-infancy) are concerned with after the death of a sibling; these questions cut across developmental differences (Papenbrock and Voss 2):

1. Did I cause the death?

2. Will I die too?

3. Who will take care of me? (especially true in parental death)

Speece and Brent (36–39) have concluded that there are a number of subconcepts in children's understanding of death, two of which are particularly important for grief ministers:

1. Causality: Why do living things die?
2. Noncorporeal continuation: What happens after death? Where does my soul go?

Gender

Chapter Three already noted how males and females *seem* to grieve differently: males are more action-oriented and seem to get through grief more quickly, and females spend more time in the second phase of grief. We can see that Hal and Louis are grieving in this way by becoming very active. We can also see that both Celeste and Tina are spending more time with their feelings. Ted is a bit of an enigma, because he seems to be withdrawing. Gender roles and expectations seem to be having an influence on how most family members are grieving.

Developmental Level [1]

Infancy: 0–2; developmental task: trust versus mistrust.[2] Children of this age cannot comprehend the concept of death, but can understand *sadness*. Parents, caretakers, counselors, teachers, and ministers need to be especially vigilant for changes in behavior, such as irritability, eating, bowel, or bladder disturbances, emotional withdrawal, and slowing of developmental abilities.

The preverbal child will need physical reassurance and the security of a constant, consistent, and loving caretaker. Verbal toddlers will need this and will also need to be reassured verbally. Two year olds will ask questions that need to be addressed simply, but directly.

Preschool: 3–5; developmental task: autonomy versus shame. At this age children think death is reversible (like E.T. and Jesus). They expect that their sibling will come back to life because death is temporary. Magical thinking may begin at this time and children may believe that they caused their sibling's death by wishing for it. Children also begin to fear that others may also die.

Watch for eating and sleeping disturbances, bodily distress, regression, fear, and guilt. We need to be especially open, understanding, and truthful; avoid euphemisms; and encourage closure. We also need to let children decide whether they want to participate in post-death rituals.

School-Age: 6–9 or 10; developmental task: initiative versus guilt. At this age, children understand that death is final. They may need great detail about the death itself. They have an image of death as a person who comes and takes them away. They are able to understand that death is real, though magical thinking is still present. They are able to more readily verbalize their feelings of grief.

They need simple, direct, honest, and accurate information; acceptance of all feelings; and a willingness to deal with the guilt caused by magical thinking. Watch for difficulties at school, poor grades, socially inappropriate behavior, and physical ailments. Children will benefit from adults talking with them about their own grief and being included in the planning of rituals.

Adolescence: 9 or 10–12; developmental task: industry versus inferiority. Adolescents are dealing with *more* of *everything*: more awareness of the finality of death, more anger, more guilt, more denial, more sadness, more confusion, and more fear of their own death. Adolescents are struggling with trying to fit in and may therefore experience difficulty in coping with the enormity of these feelings. They may feel they have to "grow up," or they may try to hide their emotions—whatever it takes to fit in with their peers, and not stand out.

Watch for rebellion, dropping friendships, drugs, promiscuity, isolation, and suicidal thoughts. Adolescents will need a combination of support and freedom to grieve in their own way.

In the Greene family, Ted falls under this category. Awareness of the developmental aspects of his grief can help Ted, the family, and the grief minister.

Teenagers: 13–19; developmental task: identity versus role confusion. We may be tempted to assume that teens can hold their own with grief; however, they still need the love and support of adults. They are still struggling between youth and adulthood. They are at a stage where they are forging their own identities while de-idealizing, and separating from, their parents. Teenagers still need to fit in with their peers. This is the age when they will grapple with the more abstract mysteries of death. Death is very real, yet also a mystery. Teens will experience mood swings from needing solitude, to acting out aggressively.

Watch for prolonged somatic effects, prolonged misplaced anger, an unwillingness to express grief, a refusal to acknowledge the death, and risk-taking behaviors such as drugs and promiscuity. Grief is experienced very intensely and teens need encouragement, support, and understanding. They may benefit from a support group of other teens.

Both Hal and Celine fall into this category.

Patterns of Communication: Grieving As a Family

Most of the literature addresses grief and loss from the perspective of the individual.[3] Yet we are all parts of families, and loss impacts us both on the individual and systemic level. According to Walsh and McGoldrick, of all our experiences in life, *death* presents families with the most painful challenges that will dramatically impact both family and outside relationships ("Introduction" xv). Coming to terms with any significant loss is the most difficult task families will face ("Loss" 1). Just as individuals face tasks in relation to grieving, families face grieving tasks. Walsh and McGoldrick identify two basic tasks for families in which patterns of communication will figure prominently (8–13):

1. **Families need to jointly acknowledge that a death or loss has occurred and to jointly share the experience of the loss or death.** For this task to be completed, *the willingness and ability of families to communicate is essential*. Families must be willing to express their feelings openly, and an environment of trust and a tolerance for diverse reactions and expressions of grief must exist. Families will need to meet as a family and talk to understand each other's grief and to put the loss into meaningful perspective. The Greene family will be unable to complete this task as long as they continue to experience and express their grief only as individuals. They will need encouragement and help to grieve together as a family.

2. **Families need to reorganize as a system, redefine themselves, and reinvest their interests and energies.** Family equilibrium has been disrupted. What once worked in defining the family

and keeping the family functioning will no longer work. Established patterns of interactions, established relationships, and established roles will need to be reexamined and realigned. To do this, families need to be flexible and cohesive. They need to avoid holding onto old patterns. One example of holding onto old patterns may come in the form of "family scripts."[4] Script theory holds that we as families tend to repeat family scenarios when experiencing similar scenarios. Families have a tendency to return to old scripts, including scripts of previous generations. The Greene family—and all grieving families— need to:

* be *aware* of their grieving script
* *decide* whether their script is healthful and helpful
* *rewrite* old scripts

The only way this can happen is for families to talk with each other about the loss and how they are coping with it. The Greene family faces additional *complications* because they are grieving a *suicide,* which in itself *overwhelms* and *overloads* the family system. It is also the *untimely* death of a young person, it is a *sudden* death, and the family (and society) will probably view the death as *preventable*—three more complicating factors.

One additional factor for families and grief ministers to be aware of is the possibility of an "emotional shock wave"—an aftershock that will occur in the extended family months or even years after the loss has occurred. The death of a parent, or the death of a child (such as in the Greene family), or the death of the head of a clan, are most likely to produce this phenomenon (Bowen 85). Awareness of this phenomenon and a willingness to watch for and talk about it are essential.

Loss of a Parent

Just as the loss of a child is the most difficult loss parents will endure, the loss of a parent is the most difficult loss children will endure. Although children who lose a parent generally receive more support than when they lose a sibling (Rando, *How to Go on Living* 200), their grief may still be complicated because:

- Children are identified as disenfranchised grievers (Doka, "Hidden Sorrow" 274)—as being seen as too young to experience grief.
- Children are also seen as "disadvantaged grievers." Reasons for this include a lack of maturity, a lack of understanding, a lack of ability to express grief, a literal interpretation of death, a lack of clarity surrounding death, a lack of reassurance, a lack of capacity to tolerate pain, the intermittent nature of children's grief, and being protected from the reality of the death (Rando, *How to Go on Living* 200–203).

We know that children *do* grieve, but that they grieve differently than adults. What is helpful to say to a child whose parent has died depends on the age of the child (see pages 82–84). It is also helpful to understand some points particular to children who are grieving the death of a parent (199–204; Walsh and McGoldrick, "A Time to Mourn" 39–40):

- Children may assume the mannerisms of the deceased parent.
- Children may idealize the deceased parent.
- Children may experience a sense of panic over who will take care of them; they fear the other parent may also die.
- There may be a regression of behavior—such as thumb sucking and bed-wetting.
- Children may begin to have problems at school.
- Children may blame themselves for the death; they may engage in magical thinking—in anger, wishing the parent dead and believing they died because of this thought.
- Children who lose the same-sexed parent in childhood may have later difficulty in parenting.
- If the death is not worked through, children may remain stuck at the age of development when the loss occurred.

A number of ways to help children at various developmental ages have already been mentioned. As pastoral ministers, we can also help in the following ways:

- Help children to plan and participate in post-death rituals such as wakes, funerals, memorial services, visits to the cemetery, and distribution of personal belongings.

- Assist with designing pre-death and post-death rituals that are appropriate for children: releasing balloons, lighting candles, writing and reciting prayers, singing songs, making murals and scrapbooks, drawing, writing a letter, and placing mementos in the casket.

- Avoid euphemisms about death. Use simple, honest, and direct language.

- Be willing to talk about the theological meaning of death in language that children can understand. Follow the children's lead, instead of using "comforting phrases" to provide meaning.

- Be available and provide consistent presence, support, and encouragement. Listen to where children are in their grief and respond to expressed needs.

- Learn all we can about children's grief so that our response is both appropriate and informed.

Bowen claimed that most ministers respond to death as if it is all the same and they are aware of only the most obvious (and I would add "ordinary") grief (86).

We as grief ministers can respond with greater knowledge, skill, and depth, if we take the time and create the opportunity to do so.

Study Questions

1. Name five ways in which the parental loss of a child is one of the most complicated grieving situations a parent will face.

2. Do you agree or disagree with the statement: Men grieve differently than women. Why or why not?

3. How do survivor guilt and magical thinking affect children grieving the death of a parent?

4. Name three things pastoral ministers need to be aware of when ministering to grieving parents.

5. How do children's developmental levels affect the ways they grieve?

6. What are the two tasks for families when facing a death or a major loss?

7. Why are children called "disenfranchised" and "disadvantaged" grievers?

8. Name three characteristics that distinguish children grieving the death of a parent.

9. How can pastoral ministers effectively minister to children who are grieving?

Practicums

1. Look at the "comforting phrases" on page 77. Which is most in keeping with your own theology? Which do you prefer and why? What phrases might you add to the list?

2. Review the description of "grieving scripts" on page 85. Write a one-page description of an early experience of loss and how you (and your family) grieved that loss. Discuss it with a partner. Then write a one-page description of a recent loss, and how you (and your family) grieved that loss. How did your grieving script differ? What would you still like to change (rewrite), and why?

3. Divide into threes. Pick a developmental age of a child. Have one person play the part of that age child, another the part of a pastoral minister, and the third an observer. Talk about a recent loss—death of a pet, death of a parent, death of a sibling, parents divorcing, or death of a friend. Talk for ten minutes and then discuss.

   • As a child, what was it like? What was most helpful to you? What were your primary concerns?

   • As a minister, were you able to relate? What helped and what hindered you? How did your knowledge of developmental ages inform you?

Chapter Five

Lingering Losses

This chapter will look at a number of illnesses that are long-term and chronic in nature: cancer, mental illness, and multiple sclerosis. These illnesses are also referred to as *catastrophic illnesses*. Any of these illnesses might eventually end in death. The types of reactions experienced and the pastoral care provided would be similar to those for losses covered in other chapters, but there will also be significant differences. Each of these illnesses could fall under such categories as ambiguous losses (Chapter One), disenfranchised losses (Chapter Two), or sudden losses within a long-term illness (Chapter Three). When the person with the illness is a child, or a sibling, or a parent, much of the material in Chapter Four may also be applicable and helpful. For instance, AIDS is talked about in Chapter Two as a disenfranchised loss; it can also be considered a fatal (terminal) illness; today it is often categorized as a chronic illness (Kastenbaum, *Society* 166), which places it in this chapter.

One concept that makes long-term illness distinctive is "shadow grief." Children whose lives are overshadowed by the illness of a sibling or a parent are referred to as "shadow children," that is, children who live in the shadow of a loved one's illness. This term also refers to bereaved parents who continue to experience the "shadow of grief" years after a child's illness. Or the term "shadow grief" may refer to grief that has been so long lasting during the sick person's life, that it becomes "like a shadow" after their death. Shadow grief is a dull, persistent ache that remains with grievers.

As stated previously, the *depth* of pain experienced in longer-term, lingering losses is just as profound and deep for survivors, as the grief experienced by survivors of sudden death. Although there is time to prepare for death, to say good-bye, to tie up loose ends, to work on relationships, and to reconcile, there are other challenges specific to the long-term nature of the illness. These will become evident in looking at three types of prolonged (more than eighteen months) chronic illnesses.

Complicated Death from Cancer

Cancer is not the death sentence it once was and survival rates for many kinds of cancer continue to improve. Twenty-five years ago when my mother was diagnosed, the word "cancer" was not even mentioned. She had a "tumor" and underwent "treatment," but my mother was never told that she had cancer. I now know that she—a lifelong smoker—had developed lung cancer that had metastasized to the brain. By the time of her diagnosis she had only months to live and was not a good candidate for the few life-prolonging treatments that existed. She lived less than three months past the day of her original diagnosis. Her ordeal with cancer was not chronic, long-term, or lingering. Today, however, many people who are diagnosed with cancer have quite different experiences.

Melinda

Melinda was first diagnosed with breast cancer when she was thirty; her children were five and ten. She felt a small lump when she was showering and immediately made an appointment with her doctor. One week later the biopsy determined that she had breast cancer. Although the cancer appeared to be contained, Melinda underwent a radical mastectomy. She didn't want to take any chances that the cancer would reappear. Her prognosis was optimistic. After surviving for five years with no signs of reoccurrence, Melinda began to feel more secure in her life. Her children were now ten and fifteen, her marriage remained intact, and her career was very satisfying. She approached her thirty-fifth birthday with feelings of joy, thanksgiving, and relief.

During a routine monthly breast exam she felt a small lump in her armpit. To her horror she found that the cancer had reappeared. The next few years were filled with chemotherapy, worry, hope, and despair. Her life and her family's life centered on her illness. Just recently Melinda was told that the cancer is now in her bones. She finds herself alternating between wanting to give up and feeling she must keep trying any and all treatments—for the sake of the children.

Melinda is your best friend and talks with you (Joyce) daily. You find yourself feeling overwhelmed—impatient, fearful, despairing, hopeful, tired, sad, and angry. You approach Alice, your pastor, asking for help. Mostly you are struggling with feeling guilty for your impatience. You are tired of Melinda's illness. It's all she ever talks about. You long for the days when you could talk about the kids, see a movie, or have a quiet cup of coffee. You find yourself avoiding Melinda's calls, visiting her less, and making excuses for not being available for her. When you call Alice, you feel as if you have reached the limit of your endurance.

Joyce 1: Hello, Alice. This is Joyce. I wonder if you could help me.

Alice 1: I will certainly try. Tell me what's troubling you, Joyce.

Joyce 2: Well, Melinda—she's my best friend—has been battling cancer for ten years now. At first I was able to be supportive and I stood by her through all the chemo and the surgeries. But lately, I am tired of her being sick. I want some time to myself. I want the old Melinda back. I don't even enjoy talking to Melinda now. And then I feel so guilty, and like I'm such a terrible person ...

Alice 2: Joyce, this is a very hard time—for you and for Melinda—and for your friendship. It might help to talk more about your feelings.

Joyce 3: But I'm so embarrassed and ashamed of my feelings!

Alice 3: That is quite normal, Joyce. Let's look at that a bit more.

Joyce 4: I'm not so sure ...

Alice 4: Joyce, maybe it would help to back up a bit. Right now you are experiencing intense feelings that are, as you put it, embarrassing and shameful. Let's see where they are coming from. Maybe we can start by you telling me a bit more about your relationship with Melinda. How did the two of you meet?

In these brief interactions we can see that Alice is trying to affirm Joyce's feelings through empathy (Alice 2) and information (Alice 3a). She also uses probes (Alice 1b, 3, and 4) to encourage Joyce to talk about very difficult and painful feelings. Response 4a is a summary, and 4b is an information question. We can also see that Alice begins to get ahead of Joyce and finds she is backing up so Joyce feels more comfortable and safer. Alice wisely reminds herself that the minister must go at her parishioner's pace.

As the conversation progressed, Alice continued to be supportive and encouraging and to share with Joyce some information about the challenges of long-term illnesses (Doka, "When Illness Is Prolonged" 6–8).

Life-threatening illnesses usually proceed through five phases.

1. *Prediagnostic phase*: There is the suspicion of a problem, and the person seeks medical advice. For Melinda this was when she found the lump and went to the doctor. This was experienced again with the discovery of a second lump.

2. *Acute phase*: There is a crisis surrounding the diagnosis, including a fear of dying and the beginning of anticipatory and actual losses. For Melinda, these losses included the loss of her breasts, her hair, her health, her ability to do everything she wanted to do, and the fear of future losses—not being there to raise her children, not being able to pursue her dreams, and not growing old with her husband. For Joyce, losses included the loss of the friendship, as she knew it; she also experienced a reversal in their roles. Melinda had always been the strong, quiet, sensitive, and "together" leader. Joyce now found herself having to assume that role.

3. *Chronic phase*: The goal is still *cure*, or at least an extension of life. Joyce felt that she and Melinda had been living through this for the past ten years.

4. *Temporary recovery phase*: The person has a period of recovery, or remission from the disease. This occurred for Melinda for the first five years. Joyce found herself unsure whether Melinda was still in this phase.

5. *Terminal phase*: Treatment shifts from cure to comfort. Joyce realized Melinda was not there yet, and that the move to this phase needed to be Melinda's decision.

As Alice described these phases to Joyce, Joyce realized that much of her difficulty came from not feeling comfortable having Melinda be *between* phases 4 and 5. As dreadful as it sounded, Joyce would prefer that Melinda definitively be in phase 5 than to remain in the uncertainty of being between phases. She could accept the certainty of Melinda's death more easily than the uncertainty of Melinda's life. For Joyce, it was the ambiguity that was so troublesome—and the uncertainty—how long could this continue? As Joyce was able to verbalize this, she found her anxiety decreasing. As she was also able to verbalize her guilt, she was able to see that her guilt stemmed from believing that she did not have the *right* to feel guilty—after all, she was not the one dying; Melinda was. In freeing herself of her self-judgments, Joyce found that she was once again able to focus on hearing where Melinda was in all this—she was probably dying! Alice affirmed that Joyce's feelings were also important and, in doing so, helped Joyce regain perspective and the ability to empathize. Alice also helped Joyce name the many losses *Joyce* had experienced—most particularly, the close, *mutual* friendship with her beloved friend. Joyce realized she had come to a point where the long-term nature of Melinda's illness was overwhelming; now Joyce needed to see if this was (also) where Melinda was with her illness.

A turning point for Joyce came with learning to redefine her relationship with Melinda. To do this she had to mourn the relationship as it had been, and come to know and relate to who Melinda was today. Although this was difficult to do, Joyce was able to accomplish it by focusing on one day at a time and by continuing to talk with Alice when she felt overwhelmed by her grief.

As Melinda transitioned to phase 5, the terminal phase, and made the decision to go on hospice care, Joyce felt more comfortable in being with Melinda and sharing her feelings with her. Up until now she was afraid she would hurt Melinda, or pressure her, or anger and upset her. Now she became very aware of the preciousness of time and the importance of even small conversations, and she was able to relate to Melinda in a new way. With the help of the hospice team, and with Alice's encouragement, Joyce was able to encourage Melinda to accept her present reality, while reminiscing about the past—two tasks of the terminal phase. She was also able to help Melinda to plan her memorial service, something Melinda's husband was uncomfortable doing.

Besides processing her feelings with Alice and the hospice chaplain, Joyce also found it helpful to continue to gain perspective and knowledge through information. The hospice chaplain was able to talk with her about the experience of anticipatory grief (see page 17,

Howard, Alzheimer's case). Joyce learned that both anticipatory grief and post-death grief involve (Rando, "Living and Learning" 44):

1. learning to accept the reality of Melinda's death, and the implications this has (Joyce felt she was doing that pretty well.)

2. revising her assumptive world by finding new ways of being and interacting that acknowledged and incorporated the ongoing changes in Melinda and in their friendship (Joyce was struggling with this, but felt she was trying to do this. After Melinda's death this would include revising her role [best friend] and identity [caretaker].)

Understanding the many complexities and complications of her grief, and being able to name what she was going through was enormously helpful to Joyce. When she realized that she was experiencing a *complicated loss* that was also *ambiguous* and *disenfranchised*, and had the added challenge of *anticipatory grief*, she felt justified in feeling overwhelmed from time to time. Joyce was also able to foresee that as much as she thought she had grieved Melinda's illness and impending death, this was all part of *anticipatory grief*, and she would need to continue grieving *after* Melinda's death (post-death grief). Now she thought she would be able to encourage other friends and family members to grieve *after* the death—that this was both necessary and helpful and part of their "grieving rights."

When death follows prolonged illness, as was true with Melinda, there are a number of factors that may continue to complicate survivor grief (Doka, "When Illness Is Prolonged" 9–12):

• the experience of the illness itself—seeing our loved one go through mental disorientation, personality change, and symptoms of disfigurement; coming to terms with the purpose and meaning of our loved one's disease

• the extent of our loved one's suffering

• the difficulties of medical decisions; after death, survivors often second-guess treatment decisions that were made, feeling guilty and wondering "what if" another decision had been made, or been made earlier

Survivors of loss from prolonged illness struggle with many of the same issues common to other types of losses. One unique factor for these survivors is the need for survivors to recapture the image of the loved one *prior* to the illness (14). This is not an easy task when the haunting image that remains is of a seventy-pound skeleton, with little or no hair, a bloated stomach, and bed sores. This imaging *needs to be done* and *can* be done through reminiscing, telling stories, and going through photographs and videotapes. Survivors may do this in an informal way or in a more formal way by incorporating it into the funeral or memorial service, and during the gathering after the final service.

Pastors or pastoral ministers can encourage this reminiscing and may be present to help facilitate conversation, bring these memories to prayer, or incorporate the stories in the memorial service or the funeral homily. We can also encourage post-death grieving and work with families to integrate the experience of their loved one's illness with their faith.

Mental Illness

Mental illness and its accompanying losses may, like cancer, also fit under the category of ambiguous loss or disenfranchised grief, and readers may need to decide which category most closely describes their experience. Naming this loss as ambiguous or lingering does not mean it is excluded from *other* categories. Part of what makes the losses in this book so difficult and so complicated is that they fit a *number* of categories and criteria for complicated grief. Because other examples were given for ambiguous and disenfranchised grief, I have chosen to focus on the long-term, *chronic* aspects of the disease for *families*.

In the United States alone, one in five people have experienced some form of mental illness, and it is estimated that one in four families are affected by serious mental illness such as depression, bipolar disorder, and schizophrenia (Goving 405). Families living with mental illness find that their loved one is *besieged* by persistent, long-term problems, and thus they are also besieged by persistent long-term grief.

Goving describes three general phases of living with mental illness (406–407):

1. *Onset*—a time of acute crisis for the person with mental illness and families; help, including pastoral care, is usually available at this time.

2. *Recovering arena*—the continuing experience of the illness; pastoral care may continue to be available, at least initially.

3. *Plateau situation*—the illness persists over a long period of time; help is available in crisis flare-ups; pastoral care is least present, and most needed here.

Cannon writes of the *grief* experienced by families (215–216):

• Grief is a *prolonged* grief, consisting of shattered dreams and changed relationships; grief remains unresolved.

• There are strong feelings of guilt and failure.

• There exist feelings of frustration, anxiety, and helplessness in the face of the unpredictability of mental illness.

The most helpful pastoral care is care that continues throughout the illness—both for persons with mental illness and for the families. Acceptance, a desire to understand, an ability to listen, openness, and presence are essential. According to John Cannon, whose son has schizophrenia, many families may not seek out care because of the stigma associated with mental illness. Therefore, pastoral ministers will need to take the *initiative* in the care. Theologically, families and ministers will together be asking, "What is God saying? How is God speaking through this situation?" As with any long-term illness, there will be anger, doubt, and questioning, and pastoral ministers will need to be comfortable staying with these feelings. Because of the misunderstandings and shame surrounding mental illness, education may be needed—for pastoral ministers and for congregations—so that awareness about the prevalence of mental illness and about our isolating attitudes toward families may be changed (218–219). Education needs to become *proactive*, rather than only *reactive*.

Rituals will be important and should be worked out *with the family*. In planning rituals with families pastoral ministers will need to look at the purpose of the ritual and determine what the ritual is attempting to accomplish. We will need to work *with* families in planning, preparing, carrying out, and reflecting on any ritual that is done.

Multiple Sclerosis

Multiple sclerosis (MS) is a disease of the central nervous system in which parts of the myelin sheath of nerve tracts in the brain or in the spinal cord become inflamed or swollen. Nutrients are not fed to the nerves and electrical impulses do not pass through as necessary. In the early stages, the disease is experienced intermittently—symptoms come and go—and in remission periods persons with MS can function "normally." Part of the difficulty in living with MS is that there is no pattern in which the attacks reoccur, but usually the attacks become more severe and more frequent. In the later stages of MS, the individual may have difficulty walking, seeing, speaking, and controlling the bladder. MS affects one out of every one thousand people and two-thirds of the people with MS are women (van der Poel 66). The symptoms of MS grow progressively worse with time.

The intermittent, unpredictable, long-term nature of the attacks, coupled with the many losses experienced (loss of various physical abilities, loss of control, loss of independence) greatly impact physical, psychological, and spiritual health. In particular, self-confidence, self-esteem, sense of value for society, faith, hope, and dreams are all affected (66).

Deanna

Deanna was thirty-five years old when she was diagnosed with MS. After her first attack, she remained relatively symptom-free for two years. Although she lived with some anxiety about her future, she had not yet experienced any debilitating effects from the disease and wondered if she had a "mild" form that would allow her to remain relatively symptom-free.

Three years after her diagnosis, she had her first really bad attack. When her symptoms subsided, she convinced herself that it wouldn't happen again. After that the attacks began to come more frequently, last longer, and grow progressively worse. She no longer lived in denial, but now struggled with what MS meant in her life. She still could not see herself in a wheelchair and tried to manage without the cane her doctor recommended.

You (Joe) are on a pastoral care team at Deanna's church. You have just received information that Deanna has had to start using a wheelchair and is despondent over this. You are asked to make a pastoral call at her home. Before you go, you talk to a friend whose wife has MS.

The following conversation takes place between Joe and Deanna:

Joe 1: Hello, Deanna. You said on the phone it was okay for me to come visit with you. How are you doing?

Deanna 1: Well, as you can see (pointing to the wheelchair), not too well. I don't know how I am going to manage!

Joe 2: If it's okay with you, we can talk more about that and see if we can come up with some ideas.

Deanna 2: I can't see how it is going to help. You can't take my disease away.

Joe 3: No, I can't. But I can help you look at some ways to help you cope with your disease.

Joe is sensing a lot of anger in Deanna. Although he thinks he understands where it is coming from, he starts to feel a bit uneasy. He needs to remind himself that in addition to listening to Deanna's story and affirming her feelings, he also needs to work with her to regain a sense of what her strengths are and how she can call upon these strengths in her illness. He realizes that this may be his only visit with Deanna, and unless he can establish a relationship and help Deanna begin to identify some coping strategies, he may not be asked to return.

Deanna 3: What do you mean?

Joe 4: Deanna, in your work as a remedial reading teacher, you are able to work with children the system has given up on. You are able to identify obstacles and work with the student to tap into inner strengths and outer resources to get through those obstacles.

Deanna 4: But learning to read is not the same as living with MS.

Joe 5: No, it's not, Deanna, but in both cases it is helpful to focus on what *can* be done, instead of on what *can't,* and to tap into inner strengths and outer resources.

This may seem a bit more directive than the type of counseling many are used to. However, Joe has already *assessed* (step 1 of crisis intervention), through his phone conversation with Deanna, that she is in crisis and that she is not functioning in day-to-day activities (part of the assessment). He is now actively intervening because Deanna is emotionally paralyzed. She is unable to move forward with necessary decisions and unable to see any desirable options for her future.

In ministering with the person with MS, it is essential to (van der Poel 81–82):

- focus on strengths
- understand the relentless nature of the disease
- help focus on what *can* be done, and not only on what *can't*

In Joe 2, 3, 4, and 5, Joe focuses on strengths and what can be done. In his preparation for the conversation and in listening to Deanna's story, he tries to understand the disease and Deanna's perception of the disease.

Pastoral ministers to persons with MS (and other serious illnesses) also need to help the person develop (van der Poel 70–71):

- a positive self-concept
- an honest understanding of strengths and weaknesses
- an accurate understanding of the illness
- an understanding of motivation in life

Pastoral ministers need to determine if the person with MS (or other serious illness) is experiencing crisis and if so, employ crisis intervention strategies: assess, intervene (minister), plan, and follow-up. (Again, Joe is doing just this throughout the conversation.)

Pastoral ministers will also need to work with the person on a new spiritual perspective. Joe was able to do this later in another visit:

Joe: Deanna, we haven't talked much about how this is affecting your faith and your relationship with God.

Deanna: It's funny you should mention that. It's hard for me to think that I am worthy of God's love.

Joe: What do you mean?

Deanna: Well, I grew up believing, and I guess I still do, that the purpose of our lives was to give service to God. And I mean *active* service—*doing* good deeds. And I can't do that anymore.

Before, Deanna viewed herself and God from the perspective of a healthy person; now she views herself and God from the perspective of a person with MS. "A person's response to God normally takes on the shape of the individual's response to life" (van der Poel 47). There is a close connection between accepting ourselves and feeling acceptable to God, between being able to *do* things for God and having value in God's eyes (45).

A colleague of mine[1] has found it helpful to ask the dying person, "What are you hoping for?" Many pastoral ministers are reluctant to ask this question, fearful that the person will answer "a cure," which is beyond our resources. Yet it is still important to ask the question. The response may be something that we *can* help facilitate, such as more time with a loved one or reconciliation with an estranged relative. We may also want to ask how we can be *helpful*. Responses may range from providing prayer and spiritual guidance to helping to arrange one more trip to the mall, or to a favorite garden. We do not know, nor can we respond to, a person's (final) desires and hopes, unless we ask!

Rituals that may be helpful in serious illnesses (such as cancer and MS) include (Zulli and Weeks 180–184):

- journaling
- meditation
- going through photographs and videotapes
- receiving sacraments: communion, baptism, reconciliation, anointing

Other rituals may be developed to fit specific needs and requests.

Study Questions

1. What is "shadow grief"? How does shadow grief complicate a lingering loss?
2. What are the five phases of life-threatening illnesses?
3. What role does anticipatory grief play in long-term illnesses?
4. Name two factors that contribute to complicating survivor grief after a long illness.

5. What are some of the characteristics of grief experienced by the family of a person with mental illness?

6. What factors make multiple sclerosis a particularly complicated loss? Name two things pastoral ministers can do in their ministry to a person with MS.

7. True or false: Sudden death results in more complicated grieving than lingering death. Give reasons for your response.

Practicums

1. Imagine that you are a family member of someone who is mentally ill, a friend of someone dying of breast cancer, or someone who was recently diagnosed with MS. What feelings are you experiencing? What are you looking for in the pastoral minister who comes to see you? How does your illness, or your family member's illness, affect your relationship with God?

2. Review Deanna's case. Imagine that she has asked you to work with her to develop a "ritual of healing." How do you respond to her request? What more information would you need to know? Outline the steps you would take in responding to her request.

3. Review Melinda's case. Melinda has died and you have been asked to speak about her at her memorial service. What do you say? How do you prepare your remarks? What part do you see your remarks playing in the post-death ritual?

Chapter Six

Caring for Grief Ministers

Those who minister to the grieving will find themselves affected by their own grief. This is true in uncomplicated grieving and even more so in complicated grieving. Grief ministry tends to elicit our own feelings about loss, and to tap into deep, often unexpected, sometimes unresolved emotions of grief. It is essential that as grief ministers we take care of ourselves and take steps to insure our own emotional, physical, and spiritual well-being. If we do not do this, we will experience distress, isolation, fatigue, discouragement, and even depression. This chapter suggests a number of guidelines that grief ministers can follow to enhance our own health, so that we can continue to enhance the health of others.

Guideline #1: Make sure we do our own grieving.

It is essential that as grief ministers we work on our own grief sufficiently. This is an ongoing process. We need to heed the words of counsel, comfort, and compassion that we are speaking to others. If we have recently experienced a particularly complicated or difficult loss that we have not grieved, we may need to take a break from grief ministry. We need to be ministered to and cared for in our grieving, just as we are ministering to and caring for others. We must accompany our desire to *do* grief ministry with a willingness to deal with our *own* grief.

Guideline #2: Continually assess and enhance our own well-being.

We do this partly by attending to our own grief. As part of God's creation, we have a responsibility to be healthy in mind, body, and spirit. This will serve as a model to those we minister to and will enhance any ministry we do. Grief ministry is very demanding work. It takes a toll on us on many levels. We will not be able to continue in this type of ministry unless we are healthy.

- *Physical health*—We need to attend to our diet and exercise. One of the reactions of grief is somatic manifestation of grief. We may experience this as grief ministers as well as grievers. Attending to and improving our physical health will help us to weather the somatic distress we may experience because of the intensity of the grief we live in. Exercise will help with the fatigue and depression we may experience in doing grief ministry.

- *Emotional health*—Just as we are attending to others' emotional needs and concerns, we need to attend to our own. We need to journal, talk with friends, see a counselor, cry, laugh, take vacations, go on retreat, and balance our lives. We need to nurture supportive ministerial relationships and mutual friendships. We need to have resources available that will provide us with both nurturance and challenge. We need to keep our personal and ministerial lives in balance, and limit our working hours. We need to be alert to our own emotional needs and be willing to seek out help when we need it.

- *Spiritual health*—A healthy spiritual life is essential to doing any kind of ministry. We need to take steps to strengthen our relationship with God and with our worshiping communities of faith. This may mean joining a new community or seeking out a spiritual guide. It may mean spending more time each day in prayer or seeking out a prayer partner.

Guideline #3: Gather grief information.

Not everyone desires or chooses to minister in grieving situations. Some of us believe that we are especially gifted in this type of ministry; some of us avoid it whenever possible. But whether we like it or not, whether we are gifted or not, because we are *human* we will find ourselves in situations with families, friends, co-workers, and parishioners, where we will be called on to provide comfort, care, and support to those who are grieving. For those of us in professional ministry, this will be an expected part of our job—whether we are pastor or religious education coordinator. People in pain don't distinguish our job responsibilities as neatly as we do.

None of us can avoid grief forever—our own or others'. *Grief will find us*. Knowing more about grief will help us with at least some of our discomfort, our uncertainty, and our insecurity. Knowing about grief cannot take away all anxiety, nor should it, but it can help alleviate our fears. By learning about the grieving process, different reactions of grief, complicated grieving situations, and resources for grieving, we will be better prepared to face and work through our own and others' grief.

This gathering of information is best done *before* we are faced with difficult grief—before we are asked to preside at the memorial service of a teenager who took his own life, or to visit with a parishioner dying of complications from AIDS. This information will help us to name what we are experiencing or witnessing and will enhance our ability to respond more appropriately. For instance, *knowing* that disenfranchised grievers will be feeling particularly isolated, or ignored, or stigmatized will help us to see that an important part of ministry to disenfranchised grievers is recognition, acknowledgment, and permission to grieve.

Guideline #4: Examine our most foundational attitudes and beliefs about grief and death.

As we educate ourselves about death, loss, and grief, we also need to become more aware of the attitudes we bring to our research and ministry and what beliefs inform us.

Attitudes. Our attitudes are often reflected in the language that we use to talk about death and grief. Judy Tatelbaum has developed an exercise with words related to death that I have modified and use in my teaching (151).

The following is a list of words related to death. As you read them put a plus sign next to ones you find positive, and a minus sign next to ones you find negative; leave the neutral ones alone. Then go back again and think of these words in relation to actual people: My father is *dead*. My husband *abandoned* me. Now look at the words again and note which ones are positive and negative, and why.

Dead	Dying
Abandoned	Suicide
AIDS	Cancer
Loss	Passed Away
Passed Over	Buried
Cremated	Gone
Murdered	Divorced
Went Away	Absent
Lost	Expired

One purpose of this exercise is to make us more aware of and comfortable with using death-related words. Another purpose is to begin to get us to look at words we have difficulty with when speaking about our own losses.

I have found that people who are most comfortable with death and loss will use words that reflect that reality—like death, died, and dead. However, I do not attempt to change a person's description of their loss experience: "She kicked the bucket. He bought the farm. She expired." I note their expression and explore what lies behind it—cultural habits, or an unwillingness to deal with the reality and pain of loss.

Beliefs. In a talk I gave in 1996, I developed the concept of "grief beliefs"—understandings we have about grief and death that have developed from our experience of loss but remain primarily unnamed. I encourage everyone to name their personal "grief beliefs," and then reflect and examine and rewrite these beliefs on a regular basis. I will cite one of my "grief beliefs" as an example. I break it down into "former" and "current" belief to show how my belief has changed through reflection, experience, and education.

Former Grief Belief: The grieving cycle takes six months to one year to complete.

I used to believe that I only needed to "get through" the first year after a loss—through the birthday, the anniversary, the holidays, and special days—just *once* without my loved one, and I would be finished with my grieving. As a good, task-oriented person, I approached grieving as just one more task to complete, one more item to clear off my desk, so I could make room for other "projects." Through the years I have found that this sometimes works, but more often this approach is a denial of the intensity of my grief, or a displacement, or a postponing, or a minimizing (Wolfert)—anything to avoid my grief. Then years later I will say to myself, or be told by a friend, therapist, or pastoral minister, "You've never really grieved that loss, have you?" and I will have to admit the truth.

I now know that there is no neat timeline for grieving and that I will grieve some losses, particularly complicated losses and difficult deaths, for the rest of my life, but that is okay. It is actually more than okay, it is necessary. This does not mean that I will be in *acute* grief, but that I will sometimes experience *STUG*—Subsequent, Temporary Upsurges of Grief—especially at significant times in my life, when something reminds me of the person or the relationship I have lost (Rando, *Complicated Mourning* 64).

Grief Belief Restated (Current): Grief, particularly complicated grief, is not something to be gotten over as soon as possible, but gotten through as best we can. Some losses will take a lifetime to grieve, and that is necessary.

On a societal level, as an American culture, our attitudes and beliefs toward death may be characterized as both death denying (Rando, *Grief, Dying and Death* 5) and death defying (Karaban, "Grief"). By publishing scores of books on grief and death, we have made them less of a taboo subject of conversation. However, we have also tended to objectify and pigeonhole death and grief as something to be studied and examined, even defied, seeing "it" as a subject to be taken along with history and algebra. In other words, although we have become more accepting of death and grief as a topic of conversation, or as an experience to be looked at, we have not adequately dealt with them on a personal, emotional level. (See Guideline #1, page 103.)

Guideline #5: Be prepared for the intimacy of sharing in another's grief.

Gathering and sharing information about grief *alone* will not make us good grief ministers. We need to also connect with grievers on an emotional and spiritual level. To do this we must remain separate enough from their story to hear their particular perspective, yet involved enough to connect with their pain. This requires that we be adept at *empathy* on both a *content* and *feeling* level (see Skills in the Appendix).

Mac

Mac was referred to me by a local agency. His beloved wife, Grace, had just died. Although she had been ill with Alzheimer's disease for many years, Mac considered her death sudden, because he understood that she would continue to deteriorate but would live for many years to come. I was forty years Mac's junior and looked fifty years younger. As I listened to his pain, I found myself calling upon my knowledge of grief and of Alzheimer's disease to respond to him. He seemed to become increasingly frustrated, and distant, as did I.

At one point he told me I couldn't possibly understand the depth of his pain because I was so young. Although I don't often *self-disclose* (see Skills in the Appendix) in my counseling, I thought this was an appropriate time to do so. I briefly shared of my father's death after a thirteen-year struggle with Alzheimer's, and my mother's death from cancer. As I spoke I saw his face soften. "Maybe you *can* understand," he told me.

Certainly my knowledge of grief helped me here. I knew that Mac's grief was very raw and that his emotions were intense. *Yet my knowledge alone was not enough here.* My *personal experience* with loss and my willingness to *share of this experience* were needed to connect us on an emotional level and to let Mac know that I could hear and appreciate his pain.

The challenge for grief ministers is to be able to draw upon our personal experience without overdisclosing and getting caught up in our own grief. If we have done our own grief work sufficiently, we should be able to do this. Still, powerful emotions may be evoked, and we will need support and supervision to deal with them outside the ministerial/counseling relationship. We may also need help in dealing with the intimacy that develops in sharing such personal, profound, and painful feelings with another. In psychological terms, we may experience *countertransference*, as we project onto the griever—because of what he represents to us—displaced feelings that belong to other relationships. Likewise we may experience displaced feelings (often anger) that are directed *toward us* because of who we represent to the griever—*transference*. An awareness of this phenomenon will allow us to appropriately deal with its effects through *immediacy* (see Skills in the Appendix) and through supervision.

Guideline #6: Know our limits. Refer when necessary.

We need to know our own limitations—as humans and as ministers. Time, training, or experience may limit us. We need to remember that we can do great harm, even though our intention is to help. Particularly in complicated grieving situations, we may need to refer grievers to professional help. However, we may continue to be involved in their lives in supportive and pastoral ways.

Many of us are reluctant to refer for a variety of reasons.

• Grievers lack financial resources for professional help.

• It is part of our job to help all who come our way.

• Grievers trust us and do not want to be referred.

• We have failed if we refer.

• We do not know where or how to refer.

It is incumbent on us as ministers to refer if it is in the best interests of grievers. This "rule" should take precedence over all our reservations. Referral can be made easier if

• we are willing to acknowledge our limitations

• we create an expectation of referral

• we have good referral resources

• we believe that referral is necessary and benefits grievers

• we see referral as additional help, rather than abandonment

• with the griever's permission, we work with the professional counselor to provide care

Grief ministers who are unwilling to refer will be more susceptible to burnout. We owe it to ourselves and to those to whom we minister to be able to refer.

Guideline #7: Know that we are not alone. God is part of all that we do and we are part of communities of faith who are all called to be compassionate and act with justice toward each other.

The most basic definition of pastoral counseling is that God's presence is actively acknowledged and called on in the counseling relationship. We are not alone in our ministry. God is always present in us and in our relationships, and it is God's healing power working through us that transforms grief's despair. For too long we have taken an individualistic approach in our counseling and ministry work. We—as Christian ministers—are called to go beyond our individualistic approaches in grief ministry to understand that grief ministry is the responsibility of all members of communities of faith.

Practicums

1. Choose any one guideline from this chapter and work on it over the next month.

2. With a partner, discuss the benefits and drawbacks of using self-disclosure in ministry relationships. (See page 108.)

3. Write and rewrite your own personal "grief belief."

4. In a small group, pick any one case from this book and talk about how and why you would refer this person to a professional counselor.

Appendix

Skills

I have used Gerard Egan's *The Skilled Helper* for the last twelve years to teach basic counseling skills. I've drawn the following list and definitions from this work (61–217), but then adapted and modified the skills.

The grief minister should be familiar with *ten* skills.

1. Empathy: nonverbal and verbal; verbal-content, feeling, and content and feeling
2. Summary
3. Focusing
4. Prompts
5. Probes: open questions, statements
6. Information questions (closed)
7. Information sharing
8. Self-disclosure
9. Advanced empathy
10. Immediacy—here-and-now, relationship, self-involving

Empathy

Empathy is the most basic skill of grief counseling. It is the ability to *understand the world from the perspective of the griever*. It is being *with* the griever through attentive *presence* and open *listening*. It is an *intimate* undertaking; the grief minister follows the griever's story so closely, she can comprehend his thoughts, feelings, and motives—from his perspective. Empathy does not mean *approval* of what the griever says or does. It is unbiased listening to *understand* what he is feeling and thinking.

This empathic understanding is *conveyed* in two ways: nonverbally and verbally.

Nonverbal empathy can be conveyed through head nodding, which encourages the griever to continue his story and conveys listening and understanding. Nonverbal empathy is helpful, but insufficient. Empathy must also be conveyed verbally.

Verbal empathy conveys that the minister understands what the griever has said. It is a way of letting the griever know she has heard him and understood what he has said.

Verbal empathy can focus on content, feeling, or content and feeling.

Content empathy focuses on the content of what was said:

Griever: I've come here to talk about the next steps in my life. My wife died three years ago and I finally feel ready to move on in my life.

Minister: You say you are ready to make some changes.

or

Minister: It's been a while since your wife died and you are ready to get on with life.

These are two possible responses. Both focus on the *facts* of what was said.

Feeling empathy focuses on *stated feelings:*

Griever: Sometimes I still feel sad to think I will never see her again. But mostly I feel I have accepted her death and am ready to move on.

Minister: It sounds as if your sadness has moved to the back burner a bit.

The minister rephrases the feeling the griever refers to in her own words, but sticks to what was said.

Content and feeling empathy focuses on *both facts* and *feelings:*

Minister: It sounds as if your sadness has moved to the back burner a bit and you are more able to look to your future.

Empathy stays with what has been said. If no feeling has been mentioned and the minister responds with a feeling, that is *advanced empathy*.

If the minister concentrates primarily on using empathy, she will not have to worry about what to say next. Her response is a restatement of what the griever said:

Minister: If I heard you correctly you said ...

Minister: It sounds as if ...

Some grief ministers find it difficult to use empathy often because they think they are interrupting the griever. Another skill that can be used, *summary*, is like empathy.

Summary

Summary is used after the griever has been speaking for a while. The minister continues to convey his understanding nonverbally, and then *summarizes* what he has heard. The intent is still to convey *understanding*. *Summary* can be used at the beginning of a session, anytime in the session, or at the end of a session. The minister is *checking out* whether he has heard the griever accurately. If he has, the griever will affirm his understanding. If his summary or empathy is inaccurate, the griever can correct the minister's understanding.

Let us imagine that the griever has been speaking for a while. The minister responds with the following *summary*:

Minister: Charlotte, you've been talking for a while now and have made a number of points. Let me see if I've understood you. Your partner has been ill for three years now. You have been his primary caretaker. You find you are usually able to cope, but lately you have been edgy and discouraged and unable to draw upon your usual resources. You want to look at what is going on with yourself, how you can continue to cope, and what new resources you might call on. How does that sound? (Or, Did I miss anything? Or, Is that accurate?)

Summary functions like *empathy* but is used less often. The purposes of both empathy and summary are to

• let the griever know she has been heard;

• check out that our understanding is accurate; and

• encourage the griever to continue on in her story.

Focusing

Focusing (Egan calls this leverage) encourages the griever to prioritize what to focus on, make some choices, and pinpoint specific areas. Using this conversation, the minister would use the skill of *focusing* and say:

- Which of these would you like to begin with?
- Which of these are most important to you?
- Which of these are most painful to you?

It is wise to let grievers focus on what they want to with a few caveats. Most of us are willing to work on easier, less painful issues first. Yet if we work on too insignificant an issue it will not help our grief or improve our life and we may become discouraged. The minister can work *with* the griever in his choice of what to focus on. *Focusing* can occur anytime in a session, but is particularly helpful after a *summary*.

Prompts

A **prompt** is a word or phrase that helps focus the griever, or encourages the griever to expand on something she said:

Griever: I guess I would say that sometimes I do feel a little angry.

Minister: A little angry?

Griever: Well, actually maybe more than a little.

Prompts repeat the griever's key words or phrases and encourage clarification or expansion.

Probes

Probes are *open-ended questions* that encourage grievers to consider new areas of thoughts, or new alternatives. *Probes* are asked to encourage clarity, exploration, or movement. A *probe* may also be a *statement* (which is actually an implied question) such as:

- Say more about that.
- Go on.
- Please expand.

An example of a question probe would be the following:

Griever: Sometimes I feel so stuck in my grief!

Minister: What haven't you tried to get out?

Griever: What do you mean?

Minister: Well, you've told me all the ways you've tried to get out. (summary) I'm wondering what you haven't tried. (probe)

Griever: I never thought of it that way before. I keep going around in circles with my tried and true ways. I hadn't considered that a new way might be what I need.

A rule of thumb with probes: Try not to use too many, and try not to use two in a row. A probe opens up a new area of thinking for the griever and he needs time to explore that area before going on to another new area.

Information Questions

Information questions are like probes, but are usually closed questions that ask factual information. They are especially helpful in assessing a crisis situation.

- How long ago did this happen?
- What are the ages of your children now?
- When was the last time you saw him?
- Would you say you want to move to a new house?

The minister needs to watch how many information questions she asks. A rule of thumb here is that the question is asked because it is important to understanding the griever's story, not to satisfy the curiosity of the minister. The griever should not feel as though he is being interrogated.

Information Sharing

Information sharing is used to convey information to the griever. This may be information about resources, or about the grieving process. *Providing information* should be used sparingly and carefully. It should not be used to push the minister's values onto the griever.

Griever: Sometimes I feel like I am going crazy. I can't sleep, and I get confused, and my chest hurts.

Minister: Katie, those are things that need to be checked out with your doctor, of course. But they are also all part of grief.

Griever: What do you mean?

Minister: Well, when we are grieving we often experience a number of physical reactions and you have just described three of them.

Griever: You mean I might not be crazy?

Self-disclosure

Self-disclosure is a way for the minister to share something of her own personal experience with the griever. An example of this appears in Mac's case in Chapter Six (page 108). Since the focus of the grief counseling is on the griever and not on the minister, *self-disclosure* should be used only if it is for the benefit of the griever. It should be brief, to the point, and appropriate. The minister will probably know if it is effective by what the griever says next.

Griever: I don't think you can really understand. Have you ever lost a child?

Minister: Many years ago I had a stillbirth. That is not the same as your loss, but it is similar.

Griever: I didn't know that. What was it like for you?

Minister: It was difficult and some days I thought I would not make it—just like you.

Griever: It helps to know that you went through something similar.

Minister: Let's talk some more about where you are now.

The minister briefly relates a similar loss and then refocuses back on the experience of the griever.

Advanced Empathy

Advanced empathy is similar to empathy. However, *advanced empathy* goes *beyond* what was stated to what is *implied*. It is based on a *hunch* that the minister has after listening to the griever for a while. It is used only after *trust* has been established in the relationship and the minister has *earned the right* to share his hunch. It is *risky* for the minister to use *advanced empathy* because the griever may become angry, frightened, or resentful—even when the minister is correct!

Griever: Sometimes I find I can do only a little each day. I wish my co-workers would be a little more understanding of what I've been through.

Minister: Sounds like you are both discouraged with your progress and upset with your co-workers.

These feelings are implied, not stated.

Griever: I *am* discouraged. But you're right. I'm also upset by the lack of support.

Minister: Upset? (prompt)

Griever: That was your word. If I were honest, I would also say I am angry.

Note that the griever came to the word "anger" on his own. I have found it helpful to allow the griever to name his own anger. I start with "softer" words like "upset" and allow the griever to add to this. Most people do not want to be told that they are angry—even if they are!

Immediacy

Immediacy focuses on the relationship between the minister and the griever. It may take three forms:

1. *Relationship immediacy* reviews the overall relationship that the minister has with the griever.

   Minister: Stan, we've known each other for quite some time now. I have a great deal of respect for you and admire your ability to persevere in difficult situations. I also appreciate your willingness to be honest with me and tell me when I have missed something.

2. *Here-and-now immediacy* focuses on what is happening between the minister and the griever at that very moment.

   Minister: Stan, I'd like to stop a minute and talk about what's happening between us right now.

3. *Self-involving statements of immediacy* are statements that are present tense, personal, and usually positive.

   - I like the way you ...

   - I'm proud of what you've accomplished since the last time we met.

Drawing Grief

Material needed: paper and crayons

Ask members of the group to draw grief. I start by asking, "What does grief look like to you?" The drawing can be done in any way they want—in colors, symbols, or pictures. Let participants know that the drawing is really for them, and that they can choose not to share it with the group, but that there will be a group sharing of the drawings for all those who wish to share. After twenty minutes ask the group to share what they have drawn, and to comment on their drawings. If the group is very large, you may have to break up into smaller groups. I find it helpful as facilitator to draw and to share.

After the sharing, I urge participants to keep their drawings and look at them from time to time. Some may want to journal about it; others may want to take it out on the anniversary of a death or loss, or when they find they are having difficulty in their grieving. Others may want to bring their drawing to prayer, either privately, or within the group.

I do this same exercise with death, asking the group to draw what death looks like to them. Sometimes I have them draw what grief looks like on one side of the paper and what death looks like on the other side.

Endnotes

Preface

1. I prefer the phrase "minister *with* the grieving" to "minister *to* the grieving" because I believe it more accurately describes the mutuality of ministry and growth that occurs in the relationship. In this book, I will use the phrases interchangeably.

Introduction

1. Therese Rando groups possible grief reactions into four categories: psychological (affects, cognitions, defenses, and/or attempts at coping), behavioral, social, and physical (*Complicated Mourning* 36–39). I have combined the social and behavioral categories and added a new category, spiritual responses. I have also drawn from Rando's comprehensive lists in describing physical, psychological, and social/behavioral responses.

2. Rando describes this reoccurrence as STUG, Subsequent, Temporary Upsurges of Grief that may occur at anniversaries, holidays, or in particular seasons (64–77).

3. Walter Brueggemann and Joyce Rupp both add a theological perspective to the grieving process. Brueggemann writes of the psalms as describing: (a) orientation—satisfied seasons of well-being (songs of guaranteed creation); (b) disorientation—anguished seasons of hurt and suffering (songs of disarray); and (c) new orientation—seasons of surprise, when joy breaks through despair (songs of surprising new life)(19–21). These seasons are similar to the seasons, or stages, of grief. Rupp writes of the benefit of praying our good-byes in loss through recognition, reflection, ritualization, and reorientation (83–93).

4. See Schulz and Alderman; Metzger; Mitchell and Anderson (84); Sunderland (34); and Feifel (24).

5. I will use the terms "grief minister" and "pastoral minister" to describe the person (lay or ordained) who provides pastoral support and care during grieving.

6. T. Rando's book *Treatment of Complicated Mourning* is one of the few comprehensive works on complicated grief. Many books, of course, have focused on particular types of complicated grieving, such as grief associated with suicide, Alzheimer's disease, the death of a child, or AIDS. This book is unique in that it addresses a variety of complicated losses from a faith perspective.

7. T. Rando prefers the term "complicated mourning" to emphasize *both* the intrapsychic work of grief and the adaptive behaviors accompanying the loss (23–25). I prefer to use the term "grieving" to denote a broadening of the term "grief" and to reserve the term "mourning" for the cultural and religious responses to grief. In this book "complicated grief," "complicated grieving," and "complicated mourning" are used interchangeably.

8. "Assumptive world" is a term Rando uses to describe the internal assumptions grievers make about the world based on their experiences, memories, needs, behaviors, and relationships (50). When a significant loss occurs it often challenges previous (old) assumptions, and grievers must adopt new assumptions.

9. Pastoral care is supportive care that we provide for each other in the context of faith communities.

10. The word "verbatim" literally means "word for word" and is used to describe a conversation that takes place between two or more people. In this book, the pastoral verbatims described represent possible conversations, but are not actual interactions.

Chapter One

1. The word "family" is used here to mean the loved ones who surround the person who is lost, dying, or dead. This includes those related by kinship and those who are considered family by close relationship.

2. See K. J. Doka ("Disenfranchised Grief" and "Recognizing Hidden Sorrow") for a thorough explanation of this type of grief. Also see Chapter Two of this book.

3. See Boss et al., for a fuller explanation of these categories.

4. See all four of Boss's works listed in the bibliography, and Boss and Greenberg, for further information on ambiguous loss, particularly in relation to families.

5. I have experienced a situation similar to this one in my own family as a daughter of someone with Alzheimer's disease, and in my profession as a grief therapist working with grieving family members. The cases in this book are drawn from both personal and professional experiences, but do not represent any one actual situation. They are composites of situations I have been involved in.

6. Genograms are used to depict information about the family and their relationships over a number of generations. Genograms map family structures so we are able to see patterns and relationships more easily. A genogram is like a graphic depiction of a family tree, usually spanning three or more generations. It is used primarily by physicians and family therapists to chart family members, relationships, and critical events.

7. Although complicated grieving situations may require professional intervention more often than uncomplicated grieving situations, the pastoral minister has an important role to play in support and healing. Too often we as pastoral ministers abdicate our role to the professional counselor who will probably not bring in the religious aspects and religious resources for care.

8. See the Appendix for a full listing and description of pastoral skills.

9. See T. Rando ("Anticipatory Grief" 14–17) for a fuller discussion of the three time foci of anticipatory grief.

10. T. Rando describes a secondary loss as "a physical or psychosocial loss that coincides or develops as a consequence of the initial loss" (*Complicated Mourning* 20–21).

11. Lament is a type of prayer found in the Book of Psalms and elsewhere in Scripture (such as Habbakkuk and Job). It is prayer in which grievers can express their grief and challenge God's silence or intervention in their lives. It may take the form of a personal lament about an individual's relationship with God (such as Psalms 3, 4, 5, 7, 10, 22, 25) or a communal lament (such as Psalms 12, 44, 58, 60, 80, 83) that addresses a communal event of loss. See Brueggemann (187,

endnote 21, and 189, endnote 41) for a complete listing of individual and communal lament psalms.

Chapter Two

1. This is a term I have coined to refer to who is seen as having the *right* to grieve, particularly publicly.

2. This is another term I have coined to refer to the entire grieving process, particularly the long intermediate reaction that involves a variety of intense emotions.

3. In this book "survivors of suicide" are defined as the family and friends who grieve the death of the person who has committed suicide. I also refer to these survivors as "grievers."

4. Parsons follows the stages of grief as outlined by Bowlby and Parkes: shock, yearning and protest, disorganization, and reorganization.

5. Actually feelings are neither positive nor negative; it is what we *do* with our feelings that may be positive or negative.

6. The term "survivor" implies that the griever has the power to actively work through the suicide; it is a term that connotes strength and hope. The term "victim" implies that the griever is powerless in the suicide; it connotes weakness and despair. I prefer the term "survivor."

7. See Grollman.

8. For a fuller discussion of these texts see Clemons (16–25).

9. Jonah is not usually included in the scriptural listings of suicides and attempted suicides. He is included here because Clemons (22) includes him and I wanted to present the fullest possible list.

10. For a fuller discussion of these and other texts, see Clemons (29–74).

11. See Grollman, for a further discussion of these concepts.

12. PWA is usually used to refer to a *person* (singular) with AIDS; I use this abbreviation to refer to *persons* (plural) with AIDS.

13. See Hoff (29–33, 79). Hoff describes the steps of crisis intervention as assessment, planning, implementation, and follow-up. I have reordered these steps and renamed implementation as intervention.

14. If pregnant women take AZT during their pregnancy, the chances that their child will be born HIV positive fall to 8 percent (Harmon 22).

Chapter Three

1. Many pastoral ministers will not feel qualified to deal with the complexities and complications of George's grief, and are correct in assessing limitations. Referral to more qualified professionals will be covered in Chapter Six as part of "Caring for Grief Ministers." For this case, I assumed that the pastoral minister is trained and qualified in grief counseling.

2. Although I am committed to inclusive God-language, I thought it more realistic to have George use exclusively male God language.

3. I define pastoral care as short-term supportive care that we as members of communities of faith provide for each other. Pastoral counseling requires more skills and training, is longer term (three to six sessions), and is usually done by a qualified pastoral minister. Pastoral psychotherapy is long-term intensive pastoral therapy done by trained professionals.

4. When we take the life of another, it is called a homicide; if the courts rule that the homicide is intentional, it is judged to be a *murder*.

5. See American Psychiatric Association (427–429), for an extensive description of conditions, symptoms, and reactions that characterize post-traumatic stress disorder, commonly known as PTSD.

6. We can do this if the person we are working with gives us permission to do so—preferably in writing—by filling out a release form that states that we have permission to talk to specific professionals.

Chapter Four

1. Marilyn Nagy did much of the work on developmental stages of grieving in 1948. She interviewed 378 children about their views of death. Most recent research refers to Nagy's work. The charts I have developed are composites of research by Schaefer and Lions, Crenshaw, and Papenbrock and Voss. The ages at each level will differ slightly; 0–3 on some charts will be 0–2 on others. The charts I have put together are not meant to be prescriptive; they are general *descriptions* of how children experience grief developmentally.

2. Some charts include reference to the developmental tasks of that age, as written about by Erik Erikson.

3. Froma Walsh and Monica McGoldrick claim that their 1991 book, *Living Beyond Loss: Death in the Family*, was the *first* to do so.

4. For further information on family scripts and loss, see J. Byng-Hall.

Chapter Five

1. This colleague, Kathie Quinlan, is the director of a two-bed home for the dying in Rochester, New York—Isaiah House.

Bibliography

American Psychiatric Association. *Diagnostic and Statistical Manual of Mental Disorders: DSM IV*. 4th ed. Washington, D.C.: American Psychiatry Association, 1994.

Anderson, H., and E. Foley. *Mighty Stories, Dangerous Rituals: Weaving Together the Human and the Divine*. San Francisco: Jossey-Bass, 1998.

Boss, P. "Ambiguous Loss." In *Living Beyond Loss: Death in the Family*, edited by F. Walsh and ·M. McGoldrick, 164–175. New York: W. W. Norton and Co., 1991.

———. "Family Stress: Perception and Context." In *Handbook on Marriage and the Family*, edited by M. Sussman and S. Steinmetz, 695–723. New York: Plenum, 1987.

———. *Family Stress Management*. Newbury Park, Calif.: Sage, 1988.

———. "Normative Family Stress: Family Boundary Changes Across the Lifespan." *Family Relations* 29:4 (1980): 445–450.

Boss, P.; W. Caron; J. Horbal; and J. Mortimer. "Predictors of Depression in Caregivers of Dementia Patients: Boundary Ambiguity and Mastery." *Family Process* 29 (September 1990): 245–254.

Boss, P., and J. Greenberg. "Family Boundary Ambiguity: A New Variable in Family Stress Theory." *Family Process* 23:4 (1984): 535–546.

Bowen, M. "Family Reaction to Death." In *Living Beyond Loss: Death in the Family*, edited by F. Walsh and M. McGoldrick, 79–92. New York: W. W. Norton and Co., 1991.

Bowlby, J., and C. M. Parkes. "Separation and Loss within the Family." In *The Child in His Family*, vol. 1, edited by E. J. Anthony and C. Koupernik, 197–216. New York: Wiley Interscience, 1970.

Brueggemann, W. *The Message of the Psalms*. Minneapolis: Augsburg Publishing House, 1984.

Byng-Hall, J. "Family Scripts and Loss." In *Living Beyond Loss: Death in the Family*, edited by F. Walsh and M. McGoldrick, 130–143. New York: W. W. Norton and Co., 1991.

Cain, A. C., and I. Fast. "Children's Disturbed Reactions to Parent Suicide: Distortions of Guilt, Communication and Identification." In *Survivors of Suicide*, edited by A. C. Cain, 93–111. Springfield: Bannerstore House, 1972.

Cannon, J. M. "Pastoral Care for Families of the Mentally Ill." *Journal of Pastoral Care* 44:3 (1990): 213–221.

Christensen, M. J. *The Samaritan's Imperative: Compassionate Ministry to People Living with AIDS*. Nashville: Abingdon Press, 1991.

Clemons, T. *What Does the Bible Say About Suicide?* Minneapolis: Fortress Press, 1990.

Crenshaw, D. A. *Bereavement: Counseling the Grieving Throughout the Life Cycle*. New York: Continuum, 1990.

Doka, K. J. "Disenfranchised Grief." In *Disenfranchised Grief: Recognizing Hidden Sorrow*, edited by K. Doka, 3–11. Lexington, Mass.: Lexington Books, 1989.

———. "Recognizing Hidden Sorrow." In *The Path Ahead: Readings in Death and Dying*, edited by L. A. DeSpelder and A. L. Strickland, 271–280. Mountain View, Calif.: Mayfield Pub. Co., 1995.

———. "When Illness Is Prolonged: Implications for Grief." In *Living with Grief: When Illness Is Prolonged*, edited by K. J. Doka and J. D. Davidson, 5–15. Bristol, Pa.: Taylor and Francis, 1997.

Dykstra, R. "Intimate Strangers: The Role of the Hospital Chaplain in Situations of Sudden Traumatic Loss." *Journal of Pastoral Care* 44:2 (1990): 139–152.

Egan, G. *The Skilled Helper: A Problem Management Approach to Helping*. 6th ed. Pacific Grove, Calif.: Brooks/Cole Pub. Co., 1998.

Erikson, E. H. *Childhood and Society*. New York: W. W. Norton and Co., 1950.

Feifel, H. "Psychology and Death: Meaningful Recovery." In *The Path Ahead: Readings in Death and Dying*," edited by L. A. DeSpelder and A. L. Strickland, 19–28. Mountain View, Calif.: Mayfield Pub. Co., 1995.

Fulton, R., and J. A. Fulton. "A Psychosocial Aspect of Terminal Care: Anticipatory Grief." *Omega* 2, no. 2 (1971): 91–100.

Glick, I. O.; R. S. Weiss; and C. M. Parkes. *The First Year of Bereavement*. New York: Wiley, 1974.

Goving, S. D. "Chronic Mental Illness and the Family: Contexts for Pastoral Care." *Journal of Pastoral Care* 47:4 (1993): 405–418.

Grollman, E. A. *Suicide: Prevention, Intervention, Postvention*, 2nd ed. Boston: Beacon Press, 1982.

Harmon, K. S. "HIV and Pregnancy." *Positively Aware* (March/April 1999): 21–25.

Herman, J. L. *Trauma and Recovery*. New York: Basic Books, 1992.

Hoff, L. A. *People in Crisis: Understanding and Helping*. 4th ed. San Francisco: Jossey-Bass, 1995.

Jones, P. S., and I. M. Martinson. "The Experience of Bereavement in Caregivers of Family Members with Alzheimer's Disease." *IMAGE: Journal of Nursing* 24, no. 3 (1992): 172–176.

Karaban, R. A. "Grief: Personal, Pastoral and Prophetic Concerns." Ayer Lecture given at Colgate Rochester Divinity School. March 17, 1996. Rochester, New York.

———. "Isaiah 63:16—64:12 Pastoral Implications." *Lectionary Homiletics* 4, no. 12 (1993): 29–30.

Kastenbaum, R. J. "Death and Development Through the Lifespan." In *New Meanings of Death*, edited by H. Feifel, 17–45. New York: McGraw-Hill, 1977.

———. *Death, Society and Human Experience*. 6th ed. Boston: Alyn and Beacon, 1998.

La Greca, D. "Anticipatory Grief from the Clergy Perspective: Presuppositions, Experience, and a Suggested Agenda for Care." In *Loss* and Anticipatory Grief, edited by T. Rando, 81–88. Lexington, Mass.: D. Heath and Co., 1986.

Lindemann, E. "Symptomatology and Management of Acute Grief." *American Journal of Psychiatry* 101, no. 2 (1944): 141–148.

Metzger, A. M. "A Q-methodological Study of the Kubler-Ross Stage Theory." *Omega* 10, no. 4 (1976): 291–302.

Michalowski, R. "The Social Meanings of Violent Deaths." *Omega* 7, no. 1 (1976): 83–93.

Mitchell, K. R., and H. Anderson. *All Our Losses, All Our Griefs: Resources for Pastoral Care.* Philadelphia: Westminster Press, 1983.

Nagy, M. A. "The Child's Theories Concerning Death." *Journal of Genetic Psychology* 73 (1948): 3–27.

Papenbrock, P., and R. F. Voss. *How to Help the Child Whose Parent Has Died.* Redmond, Wash.: Medic Pub. Co., 1988.

Parkes, C. M., *Bereavement: Studies of Grief in Adult Life.* New York: International Universities Press, 1972.

———. "Determinants of Outcome Following Bereavement." *Omega* 6, no. 4 (1975): 303–323.

Parkes, C. M., and R. S. Weiss. *Recovery from Bereavement.* New York: Basic Books, 1983.

Parsons, R. D. "Suicide Survivors' Intervention—Prevention—Postvention." In *Clinical Handbook of Pastoral Counseling*, vol. 2, edited by R. Wicks and R. D. Parsons, 638–663. New York: Paulist Press, 1993.

Rando, T. A. "Bereaved Parents: Particular Difficulties, Unique Factors and Treatment Issues." *Social Work* (January-February 1985): 19–23.

———. "A Comprehensive Analysis of Anticipatory Grief: Perspectives, Processes, Promises, and Problems." In *Loss and Anticipatory Grief,* edited by T. A. Rando, 3–37. Lexington, Mass.: D. C. Heath and Co., 1986.

————. *Grief, Dying and Death: Clinical Interventions for Caregivers.* Champaign, Ill.: Research Press Co., 1984.

————. *How to Go on Living When Someone You Love Dies.* New York: Bantam, 1991.

————. "The Increasing Prevalence of Complicated Mourning: The Onslaught Is Just Beginning." In *Dying, Death, and Bereavement*, edited by G. E. Dickinson, M. R. Leming, and A. C. Mermann, 216–223. Guilford, Conn.: Dushkin/McGraw-Hill, 1998.

————. "Living and Learning the Reality of a Loved One's Dying: Traumatic Stress and Cognitive Processing in Anticipatory Grief." In *Living with Grief: When Illness Is Prolonged*, edited by K. J. Doka and J. P. Davidson, 33–50. Bristol, Pa.: Taylor and Francis, 1997.

————. *Treatment of Complicated Mourning.* Champaign, Ill.: Research Press Co., 1993.

————. "The Unique Issues and Impact of the Death of a Child." In *Parental Loss of a Child*, edited by T. A. Rando, 5–43. Champaign, Ill.: Research Press Co., 1986.

Raphael, B. *The Anatomy of Bereavement.* Northvale, N.J.: Jason Aronson, Inc., 1983.

Rupp, J. *Praying Our Goodbyes.* Notre Dame: Ave Maria Press, 1988.

Schaefer, D., and C. Lions. *How Do We Tell the Children?* New York: Newmarket Press, 1986.

Schulz, R., and D. Alderman. "Clinical Research and the Stages of Dying." *Omega* 5, no. 2 (1974): 137–147.

Smith, W. J. "Embracing Pastoral Ministry in the Age of AIDS." In *Clinical Handbook of Pastoral Counseling*, vol. 2, edited by R. Wicks and R. D. Parsons, 679–710. New York: Paulist Press, 1993.

Speece, M. W., and S. B. Brent. "The Development of Children's Understanding of Death." In *Handbook of Childhood Death and Bereavement,* edited by C. A. Corr and D. M. Corr, 29–50. New York: Springer, 1996.

Spiegel, Y. *The Grief Process: Analysis and Counseling.* Nashville: Abingdon Press, 1977.

Staudacher, C. *Men and Grief.* Oakland, Calif.: New Harbinger Pub., 1991.

Stone, H. W. *Crisis Counseling.* Rev. ed. Minneapolis: Fortress Press, 1993.

Sunderland, R. *Getting Through Grief: Caregiving by Congregations.* Nashville: Abingdon, 1993.

Tatelbaum, J. *The Courage to Grieve.* New York: Harper and Row, 1980.

van der Poel, C. J. *Sharing the Journey: Spiritual Assessment and Pastoral Response in Persons with Incurable Illnesses.* Collegeville, Minn.: The Liturgical Press, 1998.

Walsh, F., and M. McGoldrick. Introduction to *Living Beyond Loss: Death in the Family*, edited by F. Walsh and M. McGoldrick, xv–xix. New York: W. W. Norton and Co., 1991.

———. "Loss and the Family: A Systemic Perspective." In *Living Beyond Loss: Death in the Family*, edited by F. Walsh and M. McGoldrick, 1–29. New York: W. W. Norton and Co., 1991.

———. "A Time to Mourn: Death and the Family Life Cycle." In *Living Beyond Loss: Death in the Family*, edited by F. Walsh and M. McGoldrick, 30–49. New York: W. W. Norton and Co., 1991.

Weems, A. *Psalms of Lament.* Louisville: Westminster John Knox Press, 1995.

Westberg, G. E. *Good Grief.* Philadelphia: Fortress Press, 1971.

Wolfert, A. D. "Understanding Common Patterns of Avoiding Grief." *Thanatos* (1987): 2–5.

Worden, J. W. *Grief Counseling and Grief Therapy: A Handbook for the Mental Health Practitioner.* 2nd ed. New York: Springer, 1991.

Zulli, A. P., and O. D. Weeks. "Healing Rituals: Pathways to Wholeness During Prolonged Illness and Following Death." In *Living with Grief: When Illness Is Prolonged*, edited by K. J. Doka and J. D. Davidson, 177–192. Bristol, Pa.: Taylor and Francis, 1997.

Index

abbreviated grief, 9
abortion, 50–52
absent grief, 8, 10, 16
acceptance by self and God, 100
accidental death, 58–64
acute phase (life-threatening illness), 92
adolescence developmental task, 83
advanced empathy, 112, 116–17
AIDS, 49–50, 89
Alzheimer's disease, 16–25, 35, 108
  See also illness
ambiguous losses
  due to Alzheimer's disease, 16–26
  due to divorce, 25–29
  due to rape, 70
  lack of resolution in, 13–14, 15
  lingering illness as, 94
  Naming the Beast and, 21
  perception and, 13, 14–15
  Renaming the Beast and, 22–23
  Taming the Beast and, 21–22
  types of, 7, 13–16
Andrea's story, 68–71
Anthony's story, 44–50
anticipatory grief, 23–25, 57, 93–94
assessment of crisis, 47–48
assumptive world, 59
attitudes, 105–6

beliefs.
  See faith beliefs; God; grief beliefs
Boss, P., 14, 15
Bowen, M., 87

cancer, 90–95
Cannon, J., 96
caregiving bereavement, 19
children
  death of, 7, 73–79
  death of sibling and, 80–85
  as disadvantaged grievers, 86
  grief and developmental level of, 82–84
  loss of parent by, 85–87
  magical thinking response by, 78–79, 82
  variables affecting grief in, 81–82
  See also families; parents
chronic grief, 9, 10, 16
chronic phase (life-threatening illness), 92
circle of care, 22

community of faith, 43, 49–50, 68
  See also grief ministers
complicated grief
  by PWA (persons with AIDS), 43–44
  disenfranchised grief as, 34
  due to sudden, unanticipated loss, 55–58
  gaining understanding of, 10
  reactions of, 6
complicated losses, 6–8, 10, 94
conflicted (distorted) grief, 8–9
content empathy, 112
continuing responses (uncomplicated grief),
  2–3
countertransference, 108–9
crisis intervention, 47–48
  See also grief ministers
crisis reaction, 47
culminating responses (uncomplicated grief),
  3–4

Danny's story, 75–79
date rape, 68–71
Deanna's story, 97–100
death
  attitudes and beliefs about, 107
  by homicide, 65–68
  by suicide, 35–43
  by traffic accident, 58–64
  by violence, 7, 35–39, 42, 65–66
  cancer and complicated, 90–95
  of child, 7, 73–79
  "comforting phrases" used at time of, 77
  complicated or unresolved grief associated
    with, 6–8
  developmental level and response to, 82–84
  drawing picture of, 118
  family grieving in case of, 84–85
  loss defined by factors surrounding, 7–8
  positive and negative words related to,
    105–6
  of sibling, 80–85
  traumatic, 66–67
delayed grief, 8, 10
denial. *See* shock and denial stage
detachment, 19, 23–25
developmental levels and tasks, 82–84
  See also children
disadvantaged grievers, 86
  See also children
disbelief, 1

Index

disenfranchised grievers, 34, 35
disenfranchised losses
  abortion as, 50–52
  AIDS as, 43–50
  Alzheimer's disease as, 35
  characteristics of, 33–35
  due to rape, 70–71
  lingering illness as, 94
  suicide as, 35–43
  types of, 7
disorganization stage (suicidal grief), 38–39
divorce case study, 25–29
Doka, K., 50
drawing grief, 118

Egan, G., 111
emotional shock wave, 85
empathy
  advanced, 112, 116–17
  during assessment of crisis, 47–48
  as grief minister skill, 111–13
  Taming the Beast using, 21
faith beliefs
  acceptance by self and God and, 100
  of grief ministers, 105–7
  questioning of, 60, 62
  See also God
families
  ambiguous loss by Alzheimer's disease and,
    14–15
  ambiguous loss by divorce and, 26–27
  grieving process of, 84–85
  mental illness loss and, 95–97
  ministering to PWA (persons with AIDS) and,
    44
  Naming the Beast by, 21
  Taming the Beast by, 21–22
  See also children; parents
feeling empathy, 112
female grieving process, 78, 81, 82
focusing skills, 114

gender differences in grief, 78, 81, 82
George's story, 58–64
God
  acceptance by self and, 100
  acknowledging presence of, 110
  minister's relationship with, 104
  questioning faith in, 60, 62
  See also faith beliefs
Goving, S. D., 96
Green family story, 80–82
grief
  complicated, 6
  described in terms of stages, 5
  drawing picture of, 118
  of families due to mental illness, 96
  intimacy of sharing another's, 107–9
  post-death, 24

premature detachment and anticipatory,
    23–25
  shadow, 89
  stages of suicidal, 38–39
  types of unresolved, 8–9
  uncomplicated, 1–5
  variables affecting children's, 81–82
grief beliefs, 106–7
grief ministers
  active role in mourning tasks by, 16
  ambiguous loss intervention by, 15
  avoidance of "comforting phrases" by, 77
  guidelines for, 103–10
  health of, 104
  ministering to persons with Alzheimer's
    disease, 18–21, 25
  ministering to persons who have lost a
    parent, 86–87
  ministering to parents who have lost a
    child, 79
  ministering to persons with PTDS, 67, 68
  ministering to PWA (persons with AIDS),
    44–48
  ministering to survivors of accidental death,
    59–64
  ministering to survivors of rape, 70–71
  ministering to survivors of suicide, 40–43
  necessary skills for, 113–17
  referrals to professionals by, 109
  relationship between griever and, 117
  response of to abortion loss, 52
  support of for cancer survival grief, 91–95
  support of for family of mentally ill, 96–97
  support of for persons with MS (multiple
    sclerosis), 98–100
  use of personal experience by, 108–9
  working with divorcing families, 29
  See also community of faith; crisis
    intervention
grievers
  children as disadvantaged, 86
  "comforting phrases" said to, 77
  disenfranchised, 34, 35
  gender differences in, 78, 81, 82
  referring to professional help, 109
  relationship between minister and, 117
  unrecognized (disenfranchised), 34, 35,
    50–51, 70–71
grieving process
  beliefs regarding, 106–7
  in case of Alzheimer's disease, 18–25
  in case of divorce, 27–28
  as a family, 84–85
  gender differences in, 78
  three phases or reactions during, 77–78
  See also mourning processes
grieving rights, 94

here-and-now immediacy, 117
Herman, J., 67, 68
HIV infection, 44, 46, 47, 48, 49

Index

See also PWA (persons with AIDS)
homicide death, 7, 65–66
Howard's story, 17–25, 35

illness
    anticipatory grief during lingering, 93–94
    catastrophic, 89
    death and lengthy, 7
    mental, 95–97
    redefining relationships during, 93, 94
    rituals helpful for serious, 100
    stages of life-threatening, 92
immediacy, 109, 117
information gathering, 22, 47–48, 104–5
information questioning skills, 115
information sharing skills, 115–16
inhibited grief, 8, 10
initial responses (uncomplicated grief), 1–2

Kastenbaum, R. J., 81

Lindemann, E., 23
lingering losses, 89–100
    See also illness
losses
    ambiguous, 7, 13–31
    death of child and parental, 73–79
    defined by factors surrounding, 7–8
    defined by type of loss, 6–7
    disenfranchised, 33–52
    lingering, 89–100
    of a parent, 85–87
    sudden, unanticipated, 55–71
    traumatic, 7, 66

McGoldrick, M., 84
Mac's story, 108–9
magical thinking, 78–79, 82
male grieving process, 78, 81, 82
Mary's story, 51–52
Melinda's story, 90–95
mental illness, 95–97
Michalowski, R., 65
moral issues, 22–23
mourning processes, 9, 10, 15–16
    See also grieving process
MS (multiple sclerosis), 97–100
murder death, 7, 65–66
mythic ritual, 29

Naming the Beast, 21
nonverbal empathy, 112

onset stage (mental illness), 96

parabolic rituals, 29
parent-child relationship, 73–75
parents
    loss of child by, 73–79
    loss of, 85–87
    ministering to, 79

See also children; families
pastoral ministers. *See* grief ministers
pastoral presence, 22
perception of loss, 13, 14–15
    See also ambiguous losses
personal experience of grief ministers, 108–9
Peters family story, 25–29
physical responses (uncomplicated grief), 2–3
plateau situation (mental illness), 6
post-death grief, 24
post-traumatic stress response, 57
    See also PTSD (post-traumatic stress disorder)
prayer as lament, 41
prediagnostic phase (life-threatening illness), 92
premature detachment, 23–25
probing skills, 114–15
professional help referring greivers to, 109
prompting skills, 114
psychological responses (uncomplicated grief), 1, 2, 3
PTSD (post-traumatic stress disorder), 66, 67–68, 71
PWA (persons with AIDS), 43–50

Rando, T., 9, 10, 15, 56, 59, 66
rape, 68–71
recognizing loss, 15–16, 68, 70–71, 84
recovering arena (mental illness), 96
referrals to professionals, 109
relationship immediacy, 109, 117
relationships
    between minister and griever, 109, 117
    death and parent-child, 73–75
    disenfranchised loss of unrecognized, 33
    redefined during lingering illness, 93, 94
Renaming the Beast, 22–23
reorganizing family system, 84–85
resolution of loss, 13–14, 15
restitution, 68
rituals
    for abortion loss, 52
    for community of faith, 43
    for family of mentally ill, 96–97
    helpful in serious illnesses, 100
    mythic and parabolic, 29
    spontaneous memorialization, 68
    for survivors of suicide, 41

self-disclosure skills, 116
self-involving statements of immediacy, 117
shadow grief, 89
Sharon's story, 36–38
shock and denial stage
    of abortion, 51
    of suicidal grief, 38
    of traumatic losses, 67
sibling, death of, 80–85
social/behavioral responses (uncomplicated grief), 2, 3–4

Index

spiritual resources, 29
spiritual responses (uncomplicated grief), 2, 3, 4
spontaneous memorialization, 68
Staudacher, C., 77
STUG (Subsequent, Temporary Upsurges of Grief), 107
sudden death
  by homicide, 65–68
  by traffic accident, 58–64
  as complicated loss, 7
  See also death
sudden, unanticipated losses
  by date rape, 68–71
  by homicide, 65–68
  by traffic death, 58–64
  complicated grief due to, 55–58
  eleven issues for survivors of, 56–57
  time freeze concept and, 64
suicide
  complicated loss of, 7
  scriptural passages on, 42
  social and moral stigma of, 35–36
  stages of grief associated with, 38–39
summary skills, 113
survivor guilt, 78–79, 93
survivors of prolonged illness, 91–95
survivors of suicide
  community support for, 43
  complicated grief of, 39
  coping mechanisms for, 39–40
  pastoral minister help for, 40–43
  rituals for, 41
  social stigma and, 35–36
survivors of unanticipated loss, 56–57, 66, 67, 68

Taming the Beast, 21
teenagers, grief and developmental level of, 83–84
temporary recovery phase (life-threatening illness), 92
terminal phase (life-threatening illness), 92
theological issues, 22–23
time freeze concept, 64
traffic accident death, 58–66
traumatic death, 66–67
traumatic losses, 7, 66, 67

unanticipated grief
  contributing factors to, 16
  defining, 9
  due to rape, 70–71
  due to sudden, unanticipated loss, 57–58
  recognizing loss and, 10
unanticipated losses. *See* sudden, unanticipated losses
uncomplicated grief
  continuing responses of, 2–3
  culminating responses of, 3–4
  defining, 1, 5
  initial responses of, 1–2

tasks of, 4
unexpected death. *See* sudden death
unrecognized grievers
  abortion and, 50–51
  date rape victim as, 70–71
  described, 34
unrecognized loss, 33–34
unrecognized relationships, 33, 50
unresolved grief, 8–10
verbal empathy, 112
violent death
  by homicide, 7, 65–66
  by suicide, 7, 35–39, 42
  complicated loss of, 7

yearning and protest stage (suicidal grief), 38